Diving To The Top

Diving To The Top

Leamon Cotton, Jr.

Writer's Showcase
presented by *Writer's Digest*
San Jose New York Lincoln Shanghai

Diving To The Top

Writer's Showcase
presented by *Writer's Digest*
an imprint of iUniverse.com, Inc.

For information address:
iUniverse.com, Inc.
5220 S 16th, Ste. 200
Lincoln, NE 68512
www.iuniverse.com

ISBN: 0-595-14833-6

Printed in the United States of America

To Mary, of course

When you come to a fork in the road...Take It!

—Yogi Berra

CONTENTS

LIST OF TABLES

FOREWORD

As I sat in stunned disbelief at the many great opportunities and adventures told to me by this incredibly kind and intelligent man, I continued to laugh and stare with my mouth gapped open. As the stories unfolded I heard of how the dominoes fell hard and fast. Some of the mishaps were due to moving too fast without a plan, gambling on the integrity of others, or just being good natured and soft hearted.

While I listened, the thought that continued to come to mind was "what if?"

What if…There had been more energy put into the project?

What if…There had been an honest financier and real money on the table?

What if…He had known more about his partners?

When he finished the story, I went back to work and continued to mull over what I had heard. At around eight o'clock, he came over to my desk to say goodnight and I blurted out, "you know, you have a book to write…there are lessons residing in every one of your stories." People write stories of success all of the time and explain how they achieved it, often the readers are sucked into thinking that success is just around the corner looking for them. You need to write about the stumbling blocks associated with building a business and how to deal with them. What if…everyone could learn from your "what ifs" and turn them into real success stories?

I have had a great time working with Leamon on this endeavor and waited with anticipation for each written page. I think the reader will benefit from the lessons within the following pages and hopefully get a few laughs as well. Have fun and good luck.

Andria McDowell

ACKNOWLEDGEMENTS

I would like to express special appreciation to Andria D. McDowell who was insane enough to listen to my experiences and suggest that I put some of them down on paper. I thank Andria for her friendship and generosity with her time and thoughts. I would also like to mention with approbation the encouragement and endless enthusiasm of Larry J. Aman, a friend and fellow entrepreneur. And many thanks go to my mother, Mary L. Bates, for being positive over the years and for not worrying too loud.

INTRODUCTION

There are an abundance of books on the market that are full of get rich schemes, or simply guides to lead the entrepreneur to success. I began to read these books of wisdom at an early age and after a myriad of various deals, actually found myself basking in the arena of good times. Prior to moving to Branson, Missouri I resided in Las Vegas, Nevada where I built a real estate appraisal service into a very successful endeavor. I lived in an upscale neighborhood, wore the thousand dollar suits and drove around in a BMW. Being an entrepreneur at heart I never looked at my appraisal service as an established successful business. Although I provided my services to the Federal Housing Authority, attorneys and some of the largest banks and mortgage companies in the country; to me, it was just a deal that managed to linger around for twelve years and produce a substantial income. It was just a stepping stone that would one day lead me to the Holy Grail. As always, I kept an ear to the tracks constantly listening for a better opportunity to come along.

I urge the reader to take the time to read between the lines. This book can be an invaluable guide for one to grow and prosper. It is critical, however, to know when you are well off. You will find many pearls living within some of my worst decisions, so pay attention! Those with like beliefs tend to attract each other. In this regard, the entrepreneur will constantly rub shoulders with others searching for a similar quest and many friendships will form. These friendships, however, can hold many pitfalls and as one climbs up the ladder, entrepreneurs that are down on their luck will come out of the woodwork. It is important to get out the scale and determine if you are capable of pulling them up. Also realize that it is only prudent that they take the same precaution should you become heavy.

Additionally, it is important to know that there are many wisely selfish, so-called, ass-holes that live comfortable, guilt free lives. Regardless of its exterior appeal, this option should always be considered.

When in my prime I would have suggested that you take off your shoes, kick back and enjoy this book. If you are truly an entrepreneur, I advise you to read this with your shoes on and be grateful that you still have a pair. Once again, at the risk of being redundant "know when you are well off".

THE DEAL

I met Ken several years ago when I was working on a microwave clothes dryer. This was one of the many projects that fell along the way due to the inability to secure proper funding. Ken was also plagued with the spirit of an entrepreneur, but at the time he had fallen prey to stability and was embarrassed with a real job. I had slipped up on the surface of a misplaced idea and found myself broke and sleeping in one of his spare bedrooms. Ken nursed me to health and afterwards we periodically kept in touch. I hadn't seen him in two years when, like a case of gout, he appeared out of the blue. In some cases, gout can be cured with a bowl of cherries, but Ken needed much more than small red fruit to get relief. He was emotionally limp and needed cold hard cash. It was payback time! Ken had long since given up his job and took the plunge into chasing the deal. He was attempting to market an anti-rape pendant when his dominoes began to fall. This beautifully crafted pendant was filled with artificial skunk oil and was to be worn as a necklace. The inventor was motivated to create the medallion shortly after his daughter was violently raped. While under attack, the victim was to break the pendant, which in turn would get the foul liquid all over the attacker. This odor was calculated to last for approximately two weeks and could not be removed by conventional means. The user also had in her possession another product which would eliminate the odor from her body. In essence, this would make it easier for law enforcement to capture the assailant.

Unfortunately, the pendant fell off of his girlfriend's neck and broke inside of her beauty salon. Although she tried to use the antidote, her shop was closed down for nearly two weeks due to the putrid smell. There are challenges that reside in all relationships, and at times little things tend to pile up. For Ken, this happened to be the last straw in a series of events and continuing to stay with her was not an option. Being an entrepreneur has its moments, and this was certainly one of them. If you do not have a sense of humor and are unable to laugh at the situations that you will find yourself in, then get yourself a job; this type of life is not for you. Some of the deals discussed in this book may seem unreal, but believe me they are all true. Let us not forget the millions of dollars that were made from marketing the Pet Rock.

Although my appraisal service was growing, I still considered it a job. It was a mundane day to day existence and the most I felt I could make was two hundred thousand a year. Ken had creative abilities in apparel design and over time had established related contacts. I decided to finance a side business with him. Diving boards come in many shapes and sizes. This was one of them.

After my usual 24-hour day in the appraisal business I would join Ken in materializing the dream. We formed a separate company, rolled up our sleeves and began to design sports footwear and apparel. One of Ken's contacts put us in touch with an Asian factory that also manufactured a hot selling sneaker. We decided to focus on both domestic and international markets. At the time, foreign products were in vogue in the United States and U.S. products sold very well abroad. We named our domestic product "Nouveau Riche" and the line to be sold overseas was called "US Finesse".

Our sneakers were to come equipped with a small, stylish maintenance kit that was threaded through the shoestring. This kit included an extra set of shoestrings and a small vile that carried a fluid to clean the shoe. It was just a token to help sell the product. This was Ken's idea and I was smart enough to smell the fluid. Remember! Credibility is everything. After several weeks and a few dollars from my appraisal business, the factory provided us with prototypes of our designs. At this time we were also informed that our initial minimum order would cost us two hundred thousand dollars. Although somewhat of a shock, we felt that we could negotiate terms with the factory. When the samples arrived we were proud of what we had created and received renewed energy. Now it was time to get excited about marketing concepts.

We dove in with both feet and decided to attack the market on three fronts. We formed a relationship with a marketing team out of South Carolina. This group put up the capital for an expensive, colorful, class "A" coupon booklet. The booklet was impressive and displayed our footwear along with several name brand sneakers. Our shoes were rubbing shoulders with the big boys and it appeared as if we had been on the market for many years. The concept was "Buy one—Get one free". In order to make this work we had to be able to sell the other brands and, of course, get wholesale prices. In this regard we were forced to rent a small retail space and convince the other companies that we were going to move their product. We were moving fast, shooting from the hip and writing the script as we went along. After pricing it out we had a small margin, but knew we would do fine with volume sales. The book was equipped with ten coupons and had a value to the customer in excess of five hundred dollars. The marketing group was to sell the book for twenty dollars and keep all of the proceeds. The coupons, naturally, had our name and address on them so all of the orders would come directly to us and we would enjoy our payday. Now! I had three businesses: the appraisal service, our own product line and a retail store. The appraisal service was the only entity making money. Keep in mind that this started with me helping Ken to get on his feet, so much with keeping my life simple.

In the midst of all of this activity, I was introduced to an elderly man who was a well-known trainer in the boxing industry for many years and had trained one of the most popular heavyweight world champions. For the purpose of this book I will call him Bill. He still received residuals from fights, but was semi-retired. He was a compassionate man and active in the community. He was always trying to get misguided young men off of the streets. Bill's past was extremely colorful and he had taken several teams to the Olympics. One thing led to another and we ended up forming a non-profit organization with the idea of taking another team to the Olympics. This team, of course, would be wearing our product line in front of God and everybody. Now I had another business, and added to this expense was my weekly supply of Tylenol. If your shoes are beginning to hurt your feet, I still strongly advise you to keep them on as this story is only beginning to unfold.

The third marketing concept was telemarketing. We selected a successful telemarketing firm located in an upscale business complex. In Las Vegas, there were numerous telemarketers that specialized in ripping off the public. It seemed as if the FBI was shutting one down on a weekly basis. Our selected company had been around for many years and we were convinced that it was legit. With utmost enthusiasm we proceeded to build our empire.

Las Vegas is a town that attracts risk takers and business activity is constant, lavish and bountiful. It also has a free trade zone. This zone was located in an industrial complex just south of McCarren International Airport. We were soon to meet another entrepreneur with big ideas. She was in the process of putting together an international mall. The vendors leasing her space consisted of various countries. It just so happened that representatives from the factory that were to make our shoes dropped into Las Vegas to explore the possibility of participating in the mall. Although we were aware that two hundred thousand dollars was still needed upfront to get the ball rolling, with all of the time and expenses involved, reality began to sink in and drain me of my energy. Even Ken was wearing down and we suddenly knew how NASA felt when Kennedy popped off with his bright idea about putting a man on the moon within a ten-year period. The factory representatives were open-minded and wanted to see our operation. If our marketing concept was capable of existing outside of the womb, it was possible to put up a little pocket change and establish a credit line with them. Ken tightly gripped this dim light and became excited again. I was praying for a Lee Harvey Oswald to come along and put me out of my misery. There were times when I would glance over my shoulder and reminisce the days when I was broke and down on my luck. In these quiet moments, I realized that it would have been a lot easier to have eaten crow and approach my family for money instead of sleeping in Ken's spare bedroom. The phrase "payback is hell" is true and relative; unbeknownst to me, my life was just beginning to turn on its side. I was entering into the curve.

I hope that this is all beginning to sink in. The importance of a strong business plan as a guide to keep you on track, as well as a tool to sell to lenders will be further discussed in this book. We had set up a ten o'clock appointment for the factory reps to meet with the owner of the telemarketing firm. Our product samples and the coupon booklets were already on-site and he was prepared to help us put on a first class presentation. When we collected the reps from the mall, we were informed that they had an early afternoon flight. It was nine o'clock so we decided to take a chance and find out if an earlier presentation was possible. Upon arrival I left everyone in the car to see if the owner was available. The words on the document taped to the door were brutally official and seemed to jump out at me. I began to feel weak and emaciated. It was an official notice from the FBI stating that the facility had been seized and an investigation was in process. The long walk to the car was with weak knees and I had to think of a way to dance my way out of the malady. I calmly informed everyone that the owner had a family emergency. Fred Astaire would have been impressed with my dexterity. We proceeded to our offices and presented our product and marketing concepts as best we could. Dancing is hard enough when your partner doesn't know the steps, but the dance floor can turn into a serious battlefield if your partner is in the dark and doesn't even realize that you are moving to the rhythm of the moment. I went through the two-step and the tango, and there were times when Ken's big feet were stepping all over mine. Nevertheless, the reps still appeared to be impressed. After the meeting, we dropped them off at their hotel and I told Ken the real story. I informed him that we would more than likely be interviewed, as our material was probably the first thing that the FBI agents saw when they stepped through the threshold. Ken looked worn and distraught. This lurching between euphoria and depression was beginning to take its toll on him. I was still full of vigor, but then, I had been out dancing!

My appraisal service was located in the downtown area on the second floor of a large, newly constructed office building. My office was spacious and I shared two conference rooms and a common receptionist with several attorneys and a CPA firm. I was expecting them on a daily basis, but it took a full week before Elliot Ness and the boys entered the building. I knew that we were clean, but I was more concerned about being embarrassed around the other tenants. The receptionist called me to the front and the badges were flashed just like on TV. I often wondered what kind of chemical was put in their badges that effected the atmosphere and took the oxygen out of the air. Once again it was time to dance my way out of an uncomfortable situation. My first inclination was to go into character and pass-out right there in the lobby, but I figured that Ken's reaction would be more genuine when I brought them back to our office. Thinking on my feet, I decided on another ploy. My sister majored in criminology and had been with the bureau for several years. She worked in another state and her focus was on violent crimes. I approached them acting very concerned that they were bringing me bad news about my sister. They became quickly confused, but after I explained the relationship we all began to relax. Ken had composed himself and actually appeared calm, but I could tell that he was playing the nut role. During the coarse of the interview they found us to be credible and started to look at us more as victims of the telemarketers, instead of being a part of their scheme. To top off this joyful day at the park, they left without ever explaining what the telemarketers had done to instigate this investigation.

They took our information and over the next few weeks began to make their standard phone calls. When our marketing comrades in Carolina received their call they became nervous, and even though we were found innocent, we were never able to gain their full support. We met our Waterloo, however, when the Asians received a call from the FBI. Although they verified everything as being kosher, they made us feel as if Herbert Hoover had personally placed the call and kindly informed us that we would not be receiving a line of credit. It took awhile for reality to liquefy and flow into Ken's blood stream, and in slow motion the muscles in his face began to fail him. I'm a blues lover and I have to admit that Ken's face reflected some of BB King's best work. Nevertheless, I felt his pain and out of desperation, offered him a bowl of cherries. He was locked within a very narrow perimeter and failed to see the humor. It is imperative to learn how to distinguish your psychological state from the reality in which you find yourself if you want to move forward in a positive manner.

After the drama begins to wear off and the moment has a chance to catch its breath, one begins to realize that there are still messes that need cleaning up. This usually happens after a project takes a wrong turn, as all deals have their share of residue. I was renting the retail space on a month to month basis and I was able to shut it down. I then severed relations with the companies that were to provide the brand name sneakers. Now all I had to do was to come up with a super strength cleanser. The case of "Comet" arrived shortly thereafter. Ken's father passed away and left him with a small inheritance. We departed friends and he relocated to the East Coast. Ken offered to help me absorb what had been spent, but I declined realizing that he needed it to get on with his life and I with mine.

After all of this, I was still challenged to decide what to do with the non-profit organization. Bill had been moving forward, acquired a facility, and kids were being trained with hopes of going to the Olympics. Boxing has never been one of my favorite sports and I didn't want the hassle of dealing with the teenagers. On the other hand, I didn't have the heart to abandon them or Bill, so I began to play the role of supporter. Mixing emotions with business aren't the best ingredients for being a success.

One day Bill showed up at my office in rare form. He bounced in on the balls of his feet unannounced, and was bubbling with excitement. He had found a production company out of New Orleans who wanted to do a function to raise capital for our organization. Bill not only was proficient in boxing, but was also an expert in the martial arts. Although elderly, I figured that he would probably win the fight. I had one thing going for me; I had a strong trigger finger and if I knew then what I know now, I would have pulled out a revolver and shot him on the spot. You have to understand that battlefield decisions were being made during the few moments that I could free up between stressful deadlines and the preparation of tedious appraisal reports. Introductions were made on the phone and it was decided to produce a celebrity roast at the Tropicana Hotel and Casino, similar to the old televised Dean Martin Roast. With this decided, Bill left and without a second thought I went back to work analyzing the real estate market.

I will call the owner of the Production Company "Sue". Sue desired to keep her company small. She focused on producing one or two special events a year and was capable of attracting celebrities from several industries: Hollywood, television, music and sports. She had the personality for this industry and a phenomenal sense of humor.

Celebrity functions can be chaotic and risky. Once the wheels are set in motion and commitments are made, loss of credibility with the celebrities can put one out of business if the affair is not successful. She acquired investment capital from a group of New Orleans attorneys and was able to pre-sell several of the most prestigious hotel/casinos in Las Vegas. The participation cost was two hundred fifty dollars per plate and various groups were sold whole tables that sat ten people. It was also important to sprinkle the room with other influential people (at our expense, of course) and sell advertising in the souvenir program booklet to offset the cost. Trade-outs for ads were made with airlines and limousine companies to transport the celebrities.

When Sue set up operations at the Tropicana she also had to pay all expenses for her staff (transportation, food, rooms, etc.). Celebrity schedules are always in conflict. Finding replacements for last minute dropouts constantly kept our nerves frayed and endless communication with the media to accommodate these changes in the coliseum of hype was a necessity. Once the word was out, however, celebrities seeking more exposure for themselves began calling us on a regular basis.

Adrenaline was everywhere and constantly flowed throughout the corridors. When Sue received the phone call from the renowned boxing Production Company, she was floored. They were presenting a medium level fight on the same night as our event and wanted her to change the date of our function. Previously aware of this, it had been considered and rejected as not a threat. They were charging a nominal entry fee and it was felt that the two events would attract two separate and distinct audiences. She was unable to change the date, due to celebrity work, and transportation schedules. A significant amount of capital had also been spent on print material. Sue tried to explain her predicament, but to no avail. These people didn't give themselves much room mentally. Las Vegas is a "good ole boy" town and when it comes to the bottom line, a boxing event was going to take the front seat. Sue was on the ropes and once again, we were on that slippery slope sliding toward the abyss.

Within a few days of the phone call the pre-committed hotels began to renege on their support and ticket sales began to falter. She was being blocked by the best in the business. This was the professional fight industry, and they weren't wearing kid gloves. At this time, I knew that expenses would increase due to the costs associated with having to cover our sinking butts. I made an attempt to save capital by moving Sue and her staff into my residence. I also let them operate out of my appraisal office. At this point, although a sad commentary, the problem still belonged to her. If I had been equipped with an ounce of sense, I would have left it in her hands, but I was punch drunk and fell prey to the challenge. I wanted to see it work. The kids that Bill had recruited were exuberant about the function and I didn't want to let them down. To them, reality sang that same old song only in a different key. They were accustomed to being let down and returning to the streets. I didn't want to be a culprit in a similar scenario so I made some bad business decisions and knowingly headed for the gallows. Unfortunately it didn't work, at least financially, and we were forced to paper the room by giving out complimentary tickets. Now, for those who were not aware of our hemorrhoids, the night and aura of the event were romantic and full of life.

Décor in the huge ballroom was elegant and a full-length black curtain hung as the backdrop. It was a star-studded gala with the media, some national, covering the arrival of every limousine. Some of the trade-outs for advertisement in the souvenir program booklet began to shine. We had secured tuxedos and evening gowns for the kids in our organization and their girlfriends. We went all the way with the illusion and had limousines pick them up. It was their night and the joy on their faces became our "Preparation H". The celebrities presented themselves to a packed house and gave a wonderful performance. Sue, her group of investors, and myself were now suffering from stress induced diarrhea. We knew that two thirds of the butts in the chairs had not paid a dime. Although the event was not even close to breaking even, looking on the bright side, it was a great party. The kids were inspired to move forward in their lives and we were at least able to save our credibility.

Unfortunately, some of the tables that were purchased were done so on credit and we had to wait for the payments to come in. To top that off, I found out that Sue had been working on a shoestring budget for years and needed this event to be profitable in order for her to get on her feet. With brand name people calling in everyday it never occurred to me to check her out. This was a mistake; in *every* business deal one should take the time to check everyone out as thoroughly as possible. As payments began to trickle in, she sent her staff members back to New Orleans one by one.

In the mean time, I was footing the bill for food and other miscellaneous costs. She was the last to leave and time was not my friend. Sue was Ken's replacement and it would take eighteen months for her to leave Las Vegas and for me to wake up.

In the meantime while lingering in this dream state, I realized that the profit potential and the challenge of the production industry intrigued me. I had made friends with its glitter and decided to join forces with Sue in the production business. After all, I had to get Sue on her feet and out of my living quarters. We decided to do it again. This time we would produce a special event using celebrities from the soap opera industry.

Using my money this time around, we plunged into the water. I had the bright idea of taping the event to sell to a network or cable to cover our asses. The selected location was the Aladdin Hotel and after six months we were again into the chaos. We were to use some of the members of the camera crew who filmed the well-known soap, but at the last minute their schedules changed. We got up to the ninety nine-yard line and fumbled the football. The crew that we ended up with was inexperienced and the end product was too flawed to sell to anyone. Luckily, the room again looked good and the event appeared successful. Once again, credibility was saved, but I did lose a nominal sum of money. Shortly thereafter, I received a nice letter from Ken. He was doing well and was established in the work force. I didn't tell him that I was doing penance and in reality he was still here, just in different form.

Time passed and my closets gradually filled up with Sue's clothing and belongings. She had long since sent for her apparel and the files needed to do the last function. She had officially moved in. Also, my love life was suffering. It became difficult to explain that my relationship with Sue was strictly business. She seemed to enjoy watching me squirm and I wasn't so sure that she liked the word platonic. I was true to form, however, and refused to dip my pen into company ink.

As for the non-profit organization, the celebrity roast gained notoriety and Bill began to receive support from the city and other interested parties. Because of this release of pressure, I was able to bow out gracefully and resign from the organization.

Several months had passed and I began to feel married, a thought that has terrified me ever since I've been on the planet. I was, however, able to keep myself busy and build up my appraisal service with additional clients. During the coarse of conversation Sue had mentioned a past affiliation she had with a magazine. We decided to produce an upscale anti-drug magazine called "Antidote". It seemed as if the whole country was plagued with gangs and youngsters with drug problems. It is always added fulfillment if a project is worthy and benefits the community; however, my main motivation was money. The idea was to produce it each quarter displaying a well-known figure on the cover. We found that influential people were enthusiastic about being interviewed and discussing the subject. The anti-drug phenomenon was in vogue. The rich and famous were eager to express their concerns and reflect their attitudes on how the problem could be tackled. My drug was still the "high" associated with putting together a deal and reaping financial rewards.

An immense amount of money could be made from selling ads and the contact base established from the interview, if done correctly, could be very beneficial. On the cover of our first edition was to be the owner's wife of the most successful string of hotel/casinos in the city. She not only worked hands on in the industry, but also was a pillar in the community. We forged relationships with top-notch free lance writers, psychologists and drug clinics. An impressive product began to emerge. Ad sales started out good, and then began to level off. It became more difficult for me to find the time to massage my growing appraisal service and support the magazine at the same time. I was putting in sixteen-hour days and noticed that Sue was reaching a comfort zone. She would get up long after I did and her production began to waver. We had the contents of the production ready to go to print, but were lacking advertisement. The publication had to be of good quality in order to attract prestigious patrons. Printing cost for a magazine of this quality was substantial, and I wanted ad sales to cover this expense, not my appraisal service. It came to the point where I had to give Sue an ultimatum. I gave her two months to finish the magazine, or she would have to find new living quarters.

Instead of making an all out effort to increase ad sales, the ultimatum closed in on Sue and she viewed it as additional pressure. She shifted focus on me and secured a small consulting contract with a well-known television star whose career had staggered due to the use of recreational pharmaceuticals. We were close to the finish line and with a little effort, she could have concentrated on the magazine and help make it a success. Before the two-month period had elapsed Sue grabbed her belongings and moved in with her client in Los Angeles. I felt that it was better him than me and decided to cut my losses and put one hundred percent effort into my appraisal service. Again, out came the "Comet" for the cleanup work. I returned all funds that had been collected through ad sales and began to enjoy my solitude. A few months later I saw both of them on a national television talk show. She had talent, but lacked what it took to ride the wave all the way to the beach. Her state of mind was propelling her into realities of like conditions, but then, who was I to talk?

Several years elapsed and I moved my business into a new house that I had purchased. Business was good and overhead was low by comparison to the previous years. I began to focus on helping myself; the experience was enjoyable, but the business again became mundane and stressful.

Prior to producing our first celebrity roast, I had received an assignment to appraise a recording studio owned by one of the local entertainers. I became friends with him and his manager and had invited them to attend our productions. In turn, they had also invited me to their special events. For the purpose of this story I will call him John and his manager Jackie. One evening they called on me at my residence, their spirits positive and erect. They had just returned from a place called Branson, Missouri and had secured an option on a piece of dirt that had a sales tag of one million five hundred thousand dollars. I was asked to buy in and join them in their quest to develop the property. Never having time to watch television I had missed the episode on Sixty Minutes when boom-town Branson stood up and took a bow.

I wasn't taking any chances this time around and needed to see this area for myself. Several days later I was in Branson appraising the parcel of land that my friends were so excited about. I found myself leaning toward the conservative side when appraising property of personal interest, yet my value estimate came out at two million four hundred thousand dollars. Dirt in Branson was doing tricks and my eyebrows flipped up and filled in my receding hairline. After returning to Vegas, I got out my checkbook and polished up the diving board. When in a hurry, the best thing to do is walk slow and with caution. My first response was to talk them out of a development project, to simply do a land flip and walk away with the pro-ceeds. Everyone has a dream however, and their thinking had already been crystallized with the obsession of developing and owning an elegant sup-per club with art deco decor. As they painted the word picture, I was being sucked in with every syllable. John would be performing on center stage and for years he had done extremely well in Las Vegas. Without a doubt he would be capable of attracting the right clientele to fill the room.

I recalled driving the thirty miles from the airport in Springfield, Missouri to Branson. The Ozarks, where Branson is located, consist of green, voluptuous, rolling hills and lakes. The dust from the Las Vegas desert had already begun to clear from my throat. The people were friendly and the overall personality of the town had a bustling quality to it. The local population was only three thousand seven hundred, but the area attracted approximately six million tourists annually. Entrepreneurs and entertainers were drawn to this area on an addicting basis. A large nation-ally known theme park was also focusing on the property adjacent to ours and I knew the value would increase substantially should they develop. All of these ingredients, including my burnout in the appraisal industry, helped flavor the proposal that I was being offered.

An interesting dichotomy can exist between being friends with a per-son, and being very close strangers. The camouflage will surely show itself when a business relationship is formed and the dark clouds begin to appear. A business relationship is a marriage and should you choose to take this road, I strongly urge you to spend a day in divorce court to sharpen your perspective. If you leave the courtroom with a definition of love, as being a misunderstanding between two fools, you will be a lot better off in your assessment of whom you are going to do business with. I'm not proposing that you go out and shoot your friends before they get you, as there are many business ventures among friends that nurture satisfying rewards. I am merely stating that surprises can spring up if one takes to eating apples in the dark.

John was a true professional and always performed wearing a tuxedo, which complimented his elaborate set designs and intimate lighting. Jackie was the epitome of style and had graciousness about her reminiscent of the old Hollywood movies. I really enjoyed them and we had some delightful nights on the town in Las Vegas. We formed a corporation and Jackie, after fourteen years, left her position as manager and became a partner. John was married and had a small family. Although he and Jackie were just business associates, their lives were tightly intertwined. Here is a hot tip for you! Never enter into a relationship in which two people have already solidly established. When it comes to the bottom line, you *will* be out-voted. You will never be sure if you are a partner or a prisoner.

John's long-term contract with the hotel/casino where he performed was soon coming to an end. This created an uncomfortable sense of urgency, so we all got busy. We pooled our capital and invested in designers and architects. This became very costly as all three of us were plagued with expensive taste buds. It was also enlightening to me as I finally found someone capable and willing to share the financial burden. We found a major hotel chain that agreed to anchor our endeavor. The land was to lodge the supper club, a five star hotel with restaurant, retail space and elaborate landscaping. Our only interest, however, was in the supper club. The other entities would be leased out to help service the debt. Our major challenge entailed finding the rest of the money required to exercise our

option on the land. Until this happened all of the other plans were coun-
terfeit. My experience in the real estate industry gave me a comfort level
on this particular project. One of my interns, a retired Las Vegas land
developer, brought an investor to the table. The investor owned a string of
restaurants in Las Vegas and Arizona. He also had made several trips to
Branson, but was unable to find land suitable for his needs. We offered
him two and a half acres of our land as a home for his restaurant if he
complied with our over-all theme. In turn, he would purchase the land
and give us an option for one year to give us time to fund the entire project. I spoke with this gentleman on the phone for a two-week period
before we actually met in person. The telephone rapport was comfortable
and friendly. When John, Jackie and I finally met with him in person,
however, I could immediately sense that he had a serious problem with my
pigmentation and didn't care to do business with women. The mod squad
just doesn't work in some circles.

We didn't have much time left before our option ran out and there were
people with a back-up offer in behind us. This offer also put the investor
in a precarious situation. If we lost the property, he would also lose. Rather
than blow the deal, Jackie and I waited at a fast food restaurant and drank
coffee while John met with the investor. John actually grew to like the guy.
Jackie and I decided that we would like him also if he put up the cash. At
the time, becoming whores didn't seem like such a bad deal. John and the
investor made several trips to Branson and they began to hit it off pretty
well. The only thing that really pissed me off was that I used to enjoy the
food that the prejudiced, little, bastard served at his restaurant. Here I was
once again, sucking hind tit.

John and the investor were visiting Branson and the day of reckon-
ing was near. The investor was in constant communication with his
attorney in Las Vegas trying to figure out the best angle for penetration.
Our original option was written on the standard two-page document
typically used in the real estate industry. Two days prior to closing John
gave me a call, his voice shaking with concern. The investor's attorney

had allegedly prepared a seventeen-page document that was to be faxed to Branson prior to closing. I told him that something was wrong and advised him not to sign it, that it was better to utilize the standard form. The agreement was a simple one, obtain an option similar to the one in our possession. The only difference was that the new option would expire twelve months from the date of closing. John felt desperate and was uncomfortable with my suggestion. His singing contract in Las Vegas had expired and he felt that this was literally his only alternative. I rebutted, telling him that we were dealing from a position of strength and that we should play hardball. If we were not able to exercise our option, the person with the back-up offer would end up with the property. Neither our group, nor the investor wanted this to happen. If we stood firm, I strongly felt that he would comply with his verbal agreement, not because this was the right thing to do, but because of his greed. If he reneged on his offer, we were going to lose the property anyway. So, why not go through the wall!

During the two-month period prior to closing, the investor had wined and dined John and paid for all of the trips to Branson. He made John feel comfortable and persuaded him that a mutually beneficial relationship was in progress. John was told that some minor changes were being made to the agreement. The time of the closing was closing in on him and in the eleventh hour, the agreement still hadn't been faxed. The investor convinced John that they should go on with the closing. He promised that he would sign our agreement as soon as they returned to Las Vegas. I was convinced that he had snakes in the closet and that he was choreographing the scenario using time as a pressure cooker.

John's biggest foe was that he so desperately wanted to believe the investor. He cracked under pressure and signed the property over without ever seeing the agreement that was to provide us with another option. The dynamic duo returned to Las Vegas, both in high spirits and the stall was on. Suddenly, the investor had to go out of town on other business engagements and after several weeks John finally realized that he was not the fair-haired boy that he thought he was. I was so used to trench warfare that I shrugged my shoulders and focussed once again on my beloved appraisal service.

We kept in contact periodically and decided to place a fly in the investor's ointment. The verbal contract that he had made with John to purchase the property, and provide us with an extended option was supported by correspondence that outlined the deal. Additionally, all of the trips that he and John made to Branson supported the initial intent. In the state of Missouri, a verbal contract carries a lot of weight, so we secured the services of a well-respected attorney out of Springfield who agreed to go after him. It should also be noted that the investor had put a small down payment on the land, and borrowed the majority of the million and a half. We were able to tie up the property and stop the investor from any development until the case was resolved. This, of course, made his jaws tighten because he still had to make very large monthly payments to the bank. The case would drag out for a full year and I loved every minute of it.

In the meantime, a plan was devised to lease an existing theater to get John back on stage. My efforts in this endeavor were limited. John and Jackie finally found some investors out of New York who bankrolled the leased theater. A substantial amount of capital was spent to renovate the small facility. John and Jackie moved to Branson and both purchased homes. The opening was done in grand style and Branson locals showed themselves in evening gowns and tuxedos. John's presence was plastered on billboards, various publications and at the Springfield airport. I was happy for them and as usual, my appraisal service was sitting up there along with the North Star. I made several trips to Branson to assist in various special functions and promotions. For me these events were well-needed vacations. I really enjoyed the Ozarks and began to meet a lot of nice people.

Although I was having a great time, I began to notice that John and Jackie didn't have the freedom that they enjoyed in Las Vegas. This inner prison slightly showed itself in their personalities. Their smiles were full, but stopped short of reaching the eyes. It turned out that their investors paid them a small salary and paid all of the other bills from their New York office. Any way you tried to spin it around, the result was an entrepreneur's worst nightmare. They had a job!

Several months passed and I began to receive late night phone calls from Jackie. She needed someone to talk to. There were times when she was under pressure because payroll and the paying of bills were late. In a small town the size of Branson, this was rather embarrassing, as rumors tend to spread like wildfire. Within less than a year of the opening, the payments stopped coming in altogether. Several of the other theaters in Branson had failed. The New York investors got cold feet and decided not to risk anymore capital. Jackie didn't know what to tell the employees or creditors.

All of the business obligations were in the name of the New York investors. Therefore, John and Jackie could have made a clean break out of Branson. Instead, John sold his home, moved his family into an apartment in an effort to pay the employees and some of the creditors. Some of my money was also donated to this bailout including personal assistance. There are instances in which you will be called a jerk anyway you play it, especially when it comes to creditors. If you are going to be a jerk, sometimes it's prudent to be a cheap jerk and get out of town. Some of us have a conscience, however, and a peaceful, good nights sleep can mean everything. I'm not saying to run off in the middle of the night and not pay your bills; I am saying that it is not wise to take on a burden that isn't yours. This attitude is coming directly out of my experience bag.

Jackie called me a month later to inform me that the theater was closed. They had some other investors interested, but they hadn't hooked them as of yet. She was trying to hold on to the large colorful sign sporting John's picture at the Springfield airport and asked if I could assist in this matter. It was the first thing that visitors saw when they embarked from their flight and at the time, Branson's only advertisement. The other theaters had somehow managed to overlook this prime spot at the airport. I respectfully declined. I decided to keep the money in my pocket, as the problem did not belong to me.

A few months later I received a call from the attorney who was suing my favorite restaurant person. He wanted to depose me in Las Vegas. The meeting took place in a small conference room. Seated to my left were our attorney and his assistant. The investor had polished his horns and sat directly in front of me sporting his choir boy smile. I was pleasant, and gave him my best African American stare. In reality, I was more upset with John than I was with him. I expected the investor to do exactly what he had done. After all, a snake, is a snake, is a snake. John, on the other hand, made a decision based upon personal problems, instead of what was good for the business. The investor's attorney sat to my right and became uneasy when he began to notice his client's character flaws. It took him a few moments to make his mental adjustments and then, shook it off with relative ease. He was of the knowledge that he would receive his pay whether or not he won the case. My attorney advised me not to antagonize the creep. He wanted to present a clean, credible deposition to the court. I was professional, but took any opportunity to step on his toes without messing up the shine. The meeting took hours and I was beginning to feel fatigue. When the investor stated that he had paid John one hundred thousand dollars shortly after that famous closing, fatigue shot out of the room like a bullet and I was brilliantly focused in the present. I played it off as insignificant. I didn't want to reveal that we also had a snake in our closet. Our attorney was impressed with my deposition and the paper trail that I had accumulated. He informed me that he thought we had a strong case and that our chances of winning were very good. The case was on calendar to go to court within a short period of time and a federal judge was to preside.

Now back in Las Vegas, and everywhere else for that matter, the appraisal industry was experiencing its own challenges. The industry had taken a lot of the heat for the savings & loan failures. If lenders don't make loans, they don't eat. When the appraised value isn't high enough to support the loan, the loan will not close unless a larger down payment is made. This usually upsets the homeowner. Also when this happens a lot of people go hungry: the Realtor, the Lender and the Title Company. All of this pressure returns back to the appraiser. Most appraisers just want to do their job and reflect a fair market value. Although against the law, there are times when future assignments are covertly based on the ability to close loans. For simply doing the right thing, it was possible for an appraiser to be starved out of the business. After the bailout, the appraisal industry became regulated with a myriad of rules and regulations. Every report had to be kept on file for seven years and lawsuits were rampant. Computerized market searches created another challenge. Lenders were seriously discussing cutting out the appraisal community completely by placing their own staff on computers to analyze the market. I was also receiving an increasing number of assignment requests to appraise in drug infested areas and there were moments when I feared for my life. All of this noise was making Branson increasingly attractive to me.

Our day in court was near and I was told that it would be better if I kept my pigmentation out of the courtroom. The problem that our attorney was challenged with was that our team consisted of an Italian, a Caucasian female and an African American. These three components, coupled with the mental attitude of the area had to be given weighted consideration, so I stayed in Las Vegas. Our attorney's assistant, a very intelligent and attractive lady, sat on the stand in my place and responded to questions by reading my deposition.

During the course of all of this, my intern of two years, who had introduced us to the investor, jumped the fence, became a witness for the other side and purposely blew my cover. In other words, the black mark against us was now center stage.

Ironically, I had trained him, his daughter, and his daughter's roommate in the art of appraisal. Through me, he was able to get his appraisal license. He went on to form his own appraisal service and unsuccessfully attempted to go after my clients. He did this when I was still operating, prior to my move to Branson. Word travels fast in the lending community and he was soon out of business. As convoluted, as it may seem, he became angry with me and jumped the fence. The federal judge saw right through the investor and had no problem expressing his feelings in the courtroom. Jackie called me every night with an update. Our attorney was academy award material and it was exciting to watch his theatrics. In general she felt positive, but was concerned about one juror who kept a jaundice eye on John's nationality. All parties referred to him as Bubba.

After both sides had their say, the jury went into deliberation. Everyone, including the judge and our team, thought it was an open and shut case. After a certain amount of time had passed, however, the judge did us a favor and called a mistrial. He knew that it should have taken less time and was concerned that there would be a hung jury. Afterwards, he allowed both sides to speak with the members of the jury. The jury members stated that they immediately voted in favor of our team, except for Bubba who couldn't get past John's stereotype association with Al Capone and the boys. I'm sure that my dark cloud didn't help matters much either. We opted for the next trial to not involve a jury. Having the same judge was desired, but another one had to be selected to make the final decision. We were aware that the next trial would take place several months down the road, but we were all in high spirits. We knew that after we flipped the land to one of the several interested buyers, we would end up with five hundred thousand dollars each.

I confronted John about the hundred grand that the investor said he had paid. John denied any payment and I really didn't know whom to believe. They both had an elastic attitude toward the truth. It never even came up in court, so I didn't pursue it any further. I chose to be happy with my five hundred thousand and to keep them in view at all times. I made a few more trips to Branson and decided to make the big move. I put my home up for sale, loaded all of my possessions in a big-ole truck, and got the hell out of Dodge. All of my colleagues thought that I was running a couple of quarts low, but they looked at their businesses as professional appraisal services. I was just walking away from another deal.

I arrived in free gear; my feelings, thoughts and positive mental attitude flowed into the little town of Branson. I had enough funds to last me for two years without sacrificing my lifestyle. I also brought with me a couple of quarts of arrogance. I was convinced that I had the Midas touch *on anything that I focussed on and directly controlled.* In order to keep everything afloat until the next trial, I used my connections from the appraisal industry and formed a mortgage brokerage service in Branson. I made loans and prepared business plans for many of the entrepreneurs that blew into town.

After weeks of seeing the freshness, the heat and the excitement, I finally realized the gravity of the situation. John and Jackie had been in Branson for two years and were more destitute than I had imagined. It was like having a family, which was synonymous to a root canal as far as I was concerned. A portion of my nest egg was utilized to keep them afloat. This might all seem to you as if I was in serious need of brain surgery, but considering all of the factors, the move seemed like the thing to do at the time. The main element, of course, was the five hundred thousand dollars. We had given up on the grand development plans and wanted to pursue another small theater using others peoples money of course. At this time Branson housed approximately forty theaters. Whoever was building the largest theater in town became the wonder boy on the block. The new theaters were seating between two thousand and three thousand people.

If a two thousand-seat theater was even fifty percent full, it tended to look empty. Additionally, it was mandatory for theaters to pay fees to certain organizations based on their seating capacity. Economic factors such as these become very good at putting the ego in check. Due to the number of seats located in this small haven, marketing concepts had to be well thought out in order to capture market share. We decided to focus our efforts on a small four hundred-seat facility. It would be intimate, elegant and have a bar, which was somewhat taboo in this town located in the middle of the Bible belt. Although taboo, we realized that most of Branson's customer base consisted of the same tourists that visited John's stage in Las Vegas, a large percentage under an altered state of consciousness.

Most of the tourists that visited Branson were elderly with disposable income and the majority of the businesses concentrated on capturing the bus tour market. Our biggest challenge was being able to bring in enough revenue with a four hundred-seat venue that would be profitable for all of us. We hunkered down and began to write a detailed business plan that would not only guide us, but would be strong enough to entice a venture capitalist to put up the funds.

Prior to the Branson endeavor, John and Jackie had approached me on the production of a half-hour television variety show in Las Vegas. At the time I had too much on my plate with Sue and my appraisal service, so I had declined. They went on to produce thirteen shows that were aired on late night television. The show was done tastefully and presented some of the well-known acts that performed in Las Vegas. We felt that if we produced a similar show, it would be a revenue generator for the small theater. The concept was to purchase half-hour spots to be aired nationally on cable. By purchasing the time out-right, we would control the seven minutes allocated for commercials. This would benefit us in several ways. First of all, instead of selling commercial spots, we would make our own commercials and sell our own products. The projected revenue from product sales came to an annual income of two million dollars. The show was oriented to promote Branson instead of the theater. In this regard, we could get cooperation from the city and other businesses, such as restaurants and the hospitality market. With the rapport established from promoting these entities, they would be ripe for cross marketing concepts. The beginning and ending of the show was to have a panoramic view of Branson and a performance from our theater.

We were also going to reinstate the sneaker concept, but with a different twist. I found a factory that manufactured an inexpensive, generic replica of one of the hottest sneakers on the market. We came up with a cartoon character that we called, "The Shoe-Biz Baby". We wanted to breathe life into this character by letting her become an integral part of the television show, to include some of the narration. She looked somewhat like Tweety-Bird and had large feet which, of course lodged the "Shoe-Biz Baby" sneaker. We even came up with a Shoe-Biz Baby jingle. In theory, the other theaters would buy the sneaker from us and sell it in their gift shops.

Branson is a town in which relatively unknown entertainers can be great successes if they have their own theater and are marketed correctly. We decided to sell a package deal. We would market the top three, brand name entertainers in town, and as part of the package the customer would receive a ticket to John's show at our theater. In this manner we would receive a small profit from selling tickets for the big boys, as well as our own ticket sales and fill our theater. Also included in the package was a free pair of "Shoe-Biz Baby" Sneakers. The total package was priced out to receive profit from all entities, thus creating the illusion that the sneaker was free. This concept would not only benefit us, but Branson in general. It would not only make us the fair-haired boys with the city, but also our competitors. At the end of the year our projected income was conservatively estimated at five million. Our greed threshold allowed us to be able to live on this.

We put together a good business plan and began to shop around for the funds. We found it difficult to secure capital for anything related to the entertainment industry. It was considered high risk. We not only had to overcome objections related to the failure of some of the existing theaters in Branson, but we also found ourselves in competition with other industries. Lenders were making much more money in the hi-tech arena. I read the Wall Street Journal on a regular basis and purchased a computerized database on venture capital companies and other lending sources. One of the largest scams in the lending industry relates to up-front fees. As you shop for money you will find that a percentage of these institutions will ask for a certain amount of money up-front before they will fund your project. One of the great fears in this industry is that borrowers sometimes pull their loan applications after the lender has started the ball rolling. The lender puts in time and effort and must pay staff to perform certain tasks, such as due diligence.

At times they will move funds out of various accounts and at the end of the day have nothing to show for it. To keep the borrower loyal they will sometimes ask for a commitment fee. At times this fee can amount to one or two percent of the total amount, depending on the amount that is being borrowed. If one is looking for five million, he might be asked to come up with one hundred thousand dollars. This fee will be reimbursed after closing. Although there are some companies requiring up-front fees that are legitimate, most of them are not. Also, be cautious of brokers. Some brokers are well connected and can find the money for you and naturally they will charge you a brokerage fee. There are some brokers, however, that are not connected and are strictly in the up-front fee business. You pay them, but you will never see your loan. They will find a skeleton in the due diligence process that will preclude you from qualifying. Do not fall for the up-front fee scam. This should be the first question that is asked. Walk away and continue your search. One has to also realize that just because your project is rejected, it doesn't mean that it is a bad project. There are many lenders that have their hands tied and are trying to work themselves out of their own bad loan situations. Just like entrepreneurs, lenders have an archive of war stories. You should understand their position, as you would like them to understand yours.

I rifled through the database and sent out numerous executive summaries. These summaries consist of approximately three pages and are sales tools designed to entice the lender to request your business plan. I received numerous disheartening rejections, but kept on plugging. I just needed one person to say yes. One learns a lot during these searches and they create the opportunity to adjust your package. Start-up capital can be difficult to find. We found that no one was interested in putting up funds unless we owned our own building.

We eventually found a facility in a good location. Not only would more funds have to be added to the package for renovation, but we also had to put up capital for plans and cost work-ups for the potential lender. The Mortgage Company was making a few dollars and keeping us afloat, but our demands on it were very heavy. We were purchasing the building on a contract for deed. The existing owner needed to cover his loan from the small business administration, which was close to ten thousand dollars a month. What the hell! We were damn near millionaires! We could handle this pocket change! Our payment schedule was nine thousand five hundred per month for the first six months and then the payment would go to nineteen thousand per month until the debt was retired.

There is no scientific basis as to why nervous people eat crunchy foods. Nevertheless, at the risk of being cited for disturbing the peace, we stocked up on bushels of carrots and celery and tried to chew our way through the hard times. It normally takes sixty to ninety days to get a project funded. We were banking on a lender bailout within a six-month period. Several months had past. We were beginning to sweat blood and unable to find a bone-fide lender. We had gotten pretty good at broken field running and sought after an investor who would join forces with us if he or she agreed to keep us on the map. We found a local participant who began to help us make payments on the building. Finally, the database led us to an international venture capital firm located in Minneapolis.

This company consisted of a group of attorneys and we were required to fly up north and make a presentation. They were located on the fifteenth floor of a large new building in the middle of the upscale financial district. Their offices were equipped with expensive marble, plush furniture and accessories. We had reached the big time. This group did not charge any upfront fees, but they did have a management fee schedule. We were assigned to a paralegal that worked with us throughout the due diligence process and we were billed by the hour. Every week management would review our progress and their fee was a little more than that billed by the paralegal. After all, these were attorneys.

We calculated that if it took us ninety days to close, we would expend about six thousand dollars in fees. This did not cause us any alarm, as we were excited about the fact that our project would be in constant review. After sixty days our due diligence was completed and we were called in for a pre-commitment meeting. In other words, we were there to hammer out the deal. The conference room was full of staff members and our excitement level was at an all time high. This project was a huge gamble for us and up to this point it had depleted all of our funds. I was even having trouble paying my personal rent. I felt as if I had been hit between the eyes with a hot radiator cap when they used this opportunity to ask for an up-front fee. We were told that they were moving monies from one of their portfolios and needed insurance that we would not bolt to another lender. We had been screwed by one of the best-orchestrated scams in the business. I even found myself becoming impressed with the way they played it out. Two years later the FBI busted the chairman of this organization at an airport as he was attempting to leave the country. Subsequently, the whole operation was shut down. We also found out that they had taken several rather large companies, seeking expansion capital, for a ride.

After we lost the building, financial pressure wrapped itself around our personalities and our friendship began to deteriorate. The only thing that was holding us together was the pending lawsuit. Eventually, we had our second day in court. Although I was living in the Ozarks, I was still advised to stay away from the proceedings. I was a little peaked from the prior events, but my color hadn't changed. On the weekend prior to court, our attorney broke his ankle in a skiing mishap. He arrived on a Monday morning full of "Demerol" and any other pill he could find to relieve the pain. He was in an altered state of consciousness. The new judge was not as favorable as the previous one and the investor had enough time to create rebuttals for negatives that came up in the first proceeding. Our attorney was doped up and just didn't have the Perry Mason flair that he so eloquently displayed at the first trial. With utmost regret, we lost the case. To this day when snow falls from the sky it depresses me.

During the time I've been walking among you Earthlings, I have learned to pout with the best of them. The three of us kicked, screamed, pouted and then went off of the radar screen. The Mortgage Company was turned over to the investor that had assisted us in holding on to the building. This, of course, included all of the equipment that I brought from my appraisal service. John and Jackie had a garage sale and left town without my knowledge.

I presently own a distributorship, with a local partner, that sells and installs electronic locks to the hotel industry. You should all know by now, that this is considered "a job". So as always, my ear is to the tracks looking for a better deal to come along. The next time I decide to dive, perhaps the pool will be full of water, or better yet "Cash"!

Summary

Hopefully, I have been successful in my attempt to convey what can happen when a person is in half-assed pursuit of a business venture. Now, your view of my experiences will be somewhat distorted, as I have covered a period of fifteen years within only a few short pages. If you were to read a history book that highlighted only the blunders that mankind has experienced since the beginning of time, you would envision a distorted picture of the human race in general. During this fifteen-year period, I was able to successfully close a fair share of private deals. They had few lessons to contribute however, and were therefore extracted from the story. Stay with me for a moment. Let's specifically hammer out some valuable lessons to be learned.

It is apparent that I wanted to reap the rewards of the side businesses, but I had neither the time, nor the desire to get fully involved and make an all out effort. In a nutshell, my role was to provide the start-up capital (seed money) and then, in turn, my partners were to supply the energy. This was a mistake! Although my percentage of ownership was to be equal, the deals were structured in a manner in which Sue and Ken would receive a nice salary and in return, run the day to day operations. Even in my involvement with John and Jackie, in regards to the Branson fiasco, the object of my focus became the five hundred thousand dollars that was to be received from the winning of the court case. Lesson number one: should you decide to pursue a business endeavor, it is imperative that you take the bull by the horns, get control, and watch over it as if it were your child. If you can't give it your full attention, then don't do it! You will end up having to pay child support. It should also be obvious that I had too many scenarios going on at once. When you spread your energy too thin and one thing doesn't go as planned (which inevitably will happen) the dominoes will start to fall.

A highly skilled management team is the key to any successful endeavor. A strong management team can do wonders even if the idea has limitations. In contrast, a weak management team can lead a strong idea down the dismal path of failure. When one is in the process of starting a new business it is of utmost importance to live with it, sleep with it, and eat with it. Control! Control! Control! This should be the word of the day, each hour of everyday. After the venture grows into a position of stability you can always delegate authority to other talented people.

My appraisal service was a full time endeavor. It was successful because I put in the time, energy and controlled its every move. In regards to the projects that involved Sue and Ken, I was unable to devote the required time and energy, nor did I want to. I simply wanted to be a passive partner. Neither of my associates, however, were willing to step up to the pump and put their full energy into the business. As a result, the project suffered. The project itself limped along void of stamina and, therefore, was doomed to failure from the very start. At best, I helped with the strategy and provided support, but I let Sue and Ken throw the dice. Are you reading my lips? When playing in the high stakes business arena, throw your own dice. If you play the side bet, do it with people or businesses that have already established a successful track record. Either go full throttle, or don't go at all! No matter how I try to spin it around and hide behind the skirts of time and energy, the bottom line remains the same; when the endeavors were aborted they still carried a certain amount of momentum. I had to evacuate the rental space that was used to sell the sneakers. In the case of the magazine, I had to reimburse the advertisers. I had to deal with the non-profit organization that was still breathing. My John Henry was on the signature line and I was left to do the laundry. Don't let yourself get caught in any of these traps!

Now, let me drop some knowledge on you. It's important! Whenever you decide to invest that first dollar, be prepared to get into the drivers seat and shift into first gear. As you power shift through the gears and weave your way through the obstacles that come your way, it is important to realize that it will take a certain amount of time before the reality of the moment merges with the idea you are attempting to achieve. Don't get discouraged! Downshift! Break! Accelerate, and use all of your gears! If you put in one hundred percent effort, positive results will follow.

It requires extraordinary skill and focus when one attempts to sell an idea to an investor. In a start-up business you are asking him to put his money into a piece of air that will potentially produce profits. This can be challenging, especially if your bank account is running a couple of quarts low. Most investors want to see that the entrepreneur is dedicating all of his time and effort into the endeavor. If the entrepreneur has a job in order to make ends meet, in many instances, the money source will view this as not being totally committed to the project. Remember that instability in any form will make them nervous. This might sound pretty scary, but when an entrepreneur burns the bridges behind him and leaves nothing to fall back on, the investor will feel more comfortable in parting from his funds. The investor wants to know that when challenges arrive, the entrepreneur will not buckle under pressure and flee to the security of a job.

The fear of this happening has its merits as reflected in my story involving Ken and Sue. Both of them fled and I was left holding the bag.

The entrepreneur swims in the same water as the artist, or the musician. If they are successful, society welcomes them with open arms. Failure, on the other hand, is treated in a different light. I advise the entrepreneur not to discuss business endeavors with friends or relatives if they are not supportive. Most often they will not see your dream and their reaction can be discouraging; they simply will not be able to relate to the pot of gold at the end of the rainbow. If you are on the verge of financial disaster, at most they might suggest some form of therapy. Try to surround yourself with successful people. These are the people who will understand and encourage you, especially the ones who are self-made. Constantly remind yourself that success isn't always measured by a series of linear events progressing upward. Success can also seek its form, and most often does, through various experiences. Whether they are considered good or bad, one can learn invaluable lessons from the library of experience.

The game of darts is one of focus. It can be played with a group of people, or on a solitaire basis. The idea is to throw the dart dead center to get a bulls-eye. The interesting thing about darts is the attitude of the player. When a bulls-eye is not achieved, the player, without giving it a second thought, gathers the darts and throws again. In the game of life, we tend to dedicate a certain amount of time to the darts that missed the mark. In other words, we brood, and the more energy that we devote to brooding, the longer it will prolong that which we are attempting to achieve. It is far better to immediately pick up the pieces and continue your quest in a positive manner.

Energy is neither good nor bad. Energy simply is. It is a great ally and we can utilize it to obtain positive results, or assign it to what we might consider negative.

I find it more desirable to put it to work in a positive manner, although the negative can be of great value if it teaches you what not to do.

Remember, one might trip over a log and skin his knee, but nevertheless, he got over the log.

I have been an entrepreneur for over twenty-five years and could have selected my successes to write about, however, you can go to conventional business classes to gain the knowledge that relates to a squeaky-clean business atmosphere. There are also many classes that will teach you how to sell. I make no attempt to teach you salesmanship; I'm sharing this information with you to show you how to structure. There are certain lessons that can be learned only in the back alley. Very few, if any business endeavors are without challenges and if you view your problems as challenges, you will be far ahead of the game. *It is also better to view business without any emotional handcuffs.*

People generally make their decisions and deal with other people based on their experience with themselves. In other words, if you have never been homeless you will never fully understand why I let Sue reside with me for such a long period of time. On the other hand, as stated earlier, you should take the time to know whom you are doing business with. I don't care how many impressive pictures or certificates of so-called authenticity they have hanging on the wall. Investigate with the same vigor as a lending institution. Check them out! Check everyone out as thoroughly as possible! If you find a flaw you might decide to continue anyway, but at least you would not be surprised if the flaw rises to the surface and shows itself.

It is human nature to make decisions according to our system of beliefs. If a female, for example, subscribes to a belief that reflects it more difficult for a woman to operate in the business arena, she will more than likely meet this attitude in her experience. She will attract it. This applies to everyone: the short, tall, black, white, bald, Indian, whether of Jewish or Asian decent. Basically, anything that has in the past given you a feeling of inferiority is suspect. Read the next paragraph out loud! Repeat it often!

If my worldview has limitations, then I will unload the baggage by changing the way I perceive the business world. It will cause me to act differently and walk through the door with more confidence. My decisions will be based on the business at hand instead of the social challenges that color the arena. I will then be able to present my product or service in the best light. In this regard, certain prejudices will be diluted, or overlooked, for I am operating in a world where the green back dollar reigns.

Events are always mobile, and at times an event can seem to be as solid as concrete. This is largely due to our personal interpretation, our feelings about the reality of the moment. There will be times when you feel paralyzed as you view events through the lenses of your feelings, but don't let your emotions rule the day. Learn to distinguish reality from your ever-changing emotional state. Tell yourself often that things aren't always as they appear. An entrepreneur has to be able to move events in whatever direction is necessary to achieve the goal. Once again, I am speaking in terms of control and responsibility. Once you realize that you are the one who is in the driver's seat, you will develop a sense of power. You will begin creating desired events instead of reacting to the undesirable ones. There is always another window open; you just have to seek it out. Often, it is hidden behind the curtain of a misplaced attitude. So, act don't react.

STARTING YOUR BUSINESS

One of your first steps is to determine the legal entity existence. In other words, are you going to do business as an individual proprietorship, partnership, or corporation? Some entities are more suited to the financial industry than others, and there are certain tax issues that must be considered. Consult your accountant to ascertain what will be best for you. Let us take a quick glance at some of your options. A Corporation protects the owner of a business against personal liability. There may also be certain tax advantages available, for example corporate profits from a "C" corporation do not pass through to the shareholders. Should you elect to be an "S" corporation however, you will benefit from a special tax designation, which allows for the income of the "S" corporation to be taxed to the shareholder as opposed to the corporation per se. In other words, double taxation is avoided by not having to pay income tax on corporate net income and then having to pay further tax on the dividend income that is derived from the corporation.

Another option is the LLC or Limited Liability Company. This form of legal entity is a hybrid of a corporation and a partnership. The members of an LLC are shielded from personal liability. Profits and losses may pass directly to the members without taxation of the LLC itself. An LLC is similar to a corporation because it has the following components: limited liability, free transferability, continuity and centralized management. The taxation of a limited liability company is comparable to an "S" corpora-tion. Unlike an "S" corporation however, an LLC can have an unlimited number of shareholders or "members" as they are defined in an LLC. Once again, consult with your accountant.

When starting a small business, there are two other areas in which you must pay particular attention. One is to create a track to run on by con-structing your idea into a solid business plan. The importance of a good business plan is constantly stressed throughout this book. It is just that important! *Without it you are dead in the water!* The other is acquiring an in-depth knowledge of the financial industry. Unless you are already rich, you will need cold hard cash. If you are rich, it is still better to play with the money of others and spread the risk around. In your quest for money, the financier will run your idea through the traps and try to punch holes in it. This is the best thing that can happen to you. The funding source will force you to comply with certain standards that will give you a better understanding of your venture and a better chance to succeed. We will dis-cuss these two areas separately, although they go hand in hand.

Let us first discuss the financial industry, their attitudes and what makes them tick. By dissecting this industry you will know what to expect and hopefully, certain unwarranted fears will be eliminated. After all, they don't survive very well without the entrepreneur. You are their meal ticket, as they are yours.

What Am I Looking For?

The first step in your quest to get your business funded is to ascertain what kind of funding you are seeking. This is largely determined by your present stage of evolution toward your goal. It also helps to know what the funding source is looking for. There are certain ratios and indicators that the financial industry uses to judge the potential success of your business. "See table 1."

The Various Stages of Business Financing

Seed Money

Seed money is utilized to form the legal entity existence such as a sole proprietorship, corporation, partnership, Limited Liability Company etc. It is also used for your introductory planning and market research. Seed money is needed to perform all of those tasks that are necessary to produce a viable business plan. This money is usually provided out of your own pocket, borrowed from a bank as a personal loan, or borrowed from friends, or family.

Start-up Capital

This stage of funding is utilized to actually get the business off of the ground. Because you are selling an idea, or in other words a piece of air, it is the most frustrating position to get financed. Every day lenders are under siege with new ideas ranging from the sophisticated potential moneymakers to the screwball. They have a very difficult job because many screwball ideas, such as the "Pet Rock", are also potential moneymakers. Although there are some sources who will fund this level of finance, the majority of entrepreneurs still beg, borrow, or steal from friends and relatives. Because you are selling an idea, it is imperative that you produce a strong, comprehensive business plan as a vehicle to sell your brainstorm. Putting it down on paper is your first step in materialization.

Development Stage

Once you have produced a prototype, feasibility study, or other instrument proving that your idea can work, you are in the development stage.

This round of financing is easier to acquire than the two preceding stages. Your best ally is a strong business plan that will show, in detail, how your product can successfully penetrate the marketplace at a profit.

Mezzanine Financing

At this level your company has realized a degree of success and is near the break-even point. Maturing companies are always looking for money to expand their operation. They are in need of capital to bridge the gap to get to the next level. Although the financial industry will have a welcome mat out for these companies, they will still expect to see an extensive report that shows the company's history, financial projections, and an overview of the industry. It could be a matter of updating and adjusting your original business plan. For obvious reasons, mezzanine financing is also referred to as bridge financing.

Growth Stage

If your company is in fourth gear and generating profits it is in the growth stage. It is beyond the break-even point and the possibility of going public is a realistic option. The financier will probably seek out additional product introduction and take another look at the market to make sure that the prosperity will persevere.

Should I Borrow From Family and Friends?

If you are an honest person and believe that you have a good idea, don't be afraid to borrow money for your project. If you are in the early stages of financing and must approach family members or friends, there are certain precautions that should be considered. Those who are close to you will not take you through the snake pits that an institutional funder will. Most of them will not even know the right questions to ask. If you lose their money, it could cause a strain on the relationship for years to come, if not indefinitely. Should this be the path that you must take, I strongly suggest that you take your business plan to several traditional financiers first and get turned down. This exercise will give you insight on the quality of your project and you shouldn't be discouraged because your goal is to use the professionals as a vehicle to polish up your act. Take heed to the reasons why you are being turned down, follow their suggestions and adjust your plan accordingly. When you feel comfortable with your project, go to family and friends and take the plunge.

THE FINANCIAL INDUSTRY

You should be aware of the types of financing available to you, and also know the institutions that offer them. If you are going to play this game, you must understand how the collectors of arms, legs, and first-born children operate. This knowledge will affect your ability to get financing. Always remember that the funding source is in business to make money; and the amount that they will charge you will depend on the risk/reward ratio. The more risk associated with your project will result in you paying a higher interest rate, or giving up more equity ownership to the investor.

The lender/investor will evaluate the upside potential of your project, as well as the downside risks. The upside potential addresses the kind of profits your project can potentially generate. In other words, how much money can both the funding source and the entrepreneur make? The downside risk is usually under camouflage to the entrepreneur. In order for him to pursue his venture at all, he must have a positive mental attitude. The funding source will not be so optimistic, however, and will want to know what the liquidation value would be should the business fail. In other words, what is going to be left on the table for the investor? Your business plan should address both sides of the coin and give the lender/investor confidence that your business will succeed. The sweatier his palms, the more equity ownership you will have to give up. Outlining the downside risks in you plan shows the lender/investor that you are realistic and are capable of handling challenges as they arise.

Equity or Leveraged Lender?

It is also important that you know the difference between an equity lender and one that is leveraged. In fact, this should be one of the first questions that you ask the funding source. An equity lender has not borrowed any of their money. They use their own money, or the equity from their stockholders to purchase stock (common or preferred), or other equity securities in your business. Banks are leveraged lenders and do not fall into this category. The leveraged lender is an entity that has borrowed a substantial amount of money from either private sources, or the government. The money is borrowed at a certain interest rate and then lent out to businesses at a higher interest rate. In this regard, a leveraged lender has to either make loans, or convertible debentures. A convertible debenture is simply a loan that is convertible into common stock.

If the financial projections in your business plan fail to show immediate cash flow, the leveraged lender will not be interested in your project. Remember that he must make interest payments on the money that he has borrowed. He will also turn away from involvement in the Research and Development field.

The following section illustrates the characteristics of the common types of funding sources.

Banks

The first thing that a bank wants to determine is if one has the ability to pay back the loan. Banks make loans when risk is almost non-existent. If you have good credit and substantial collateral you can secure a personal loan as a vehicle to fund your project. If you are going to dedicate one hundred percent of your time to the business and your projections don't show a cash flow for several months, you will get little response from the bank. I know of instances where entrepreneurs secured bank loans before they quit their day jobs, but this activity is generally frowned upon. Although they do not generally lend for start-up businesses, banks and commercial finance companies are usually the first stops one makes when shopping for capital.

Banks usually offer two basic types of loans, short-term and long-term. The short-term loans will generally reach maturity in twelve months or less. They usually include lines of credit, loans for working capital and accounts receivable loans. The long-term loans generally range from one to seven years. Equipment purchases, vehicles and other major business expenses usually fall under this category. A revolving credit card can also be a good option for seed money. Banks are portfolio lenders. In other words, when they make a loan they don't sell it on the secondary market; it is put on the shelf so to speak. It is possible that a bank has already made several loans and, therefore, has a gaping hole in its purse. If this is the case, the money is tied up until some of the loans are paid off. If you get rejected and feel that you deserve a loan, take this into consideration and keep shopping. Banks have their hands tied with laws that prevent them from owning stock in a small business. Many banks, however, have established subsidiaries or venture capital companies that enable them to participate in equity based financing. The venture capital industry is discussed later in this book.

Small Business Administration

If your bank finds your collateral a little weak, take a stroll down to the Small Business Administration. This government agency will guarantee the bank loan if you fit within certain parameters. The loan guarantee loosens the bank's handcuffs and enables them to relax some of their standard criteria. Your bank may already be a preferred lender with the SBA. If so, you should ask them about an SBA loan.

The SBA has offices throughout the United States. You can call the SBA Answer Desk at 1-800-U-ASK-SBA. You can also obtain a copy of The Resource directory for small Business Management, a listing of for-sale publications and videotapes by calling your local SBA office or the SBA Answer Desk. Don't be shy, it's free.

The SBA also has a Pre-qualification Pilot Loan Program. It uses intermediaries to assist prospective borrowers in the preparation of loan application packages and the securing of loans. Give it a shot! The more knowledgeable you are about different areas of financing, the more equipped you will be in the building of your business. I must warn you, however, to be prepared as the SBA's minimum requirements can also cause you grief. The SBA doesn't like to lose money either, but stick around! There are other options.

SBA Express

For those of you who are not going after the billion-dollar sure thing, the SBA Express makes it easier for lenders to provide small business loans of $150,000 or less. Lenders are allowed to use their own forms and processing procedures to approve loans guaranteed by the

SBA. The SBA usually responds within 36 hours of receiving your completed application. Lenders may approve unsecured lines of credit up to $25,000 with SBA Express, whereas SBA's general policy requires guaranteed loans to be fully secured. Now I'm going to poke you in the eye! SBA Express loans have size standards that are based on the average number of employees over the preceding twelve months, or the average sales over the previous three years. Size standards are published for specific standard industrial classification (SIC) codes: "See table 2."

For those of you who have been carrying your dreams around in your brief case and need other avenues, keep reading.

Small Business Investment Companies (SBIC's)

These privately owned and managed investment firms (SBIC's) are licensed and regulated by the SBA. They provide venture capital and start-up financing to small businesses. **Let's snoop around a bit and see what they require.**

These companies supply equity capital, long-term loans and management assistance to qualifying small businesses. Some SBIC's (the ones that play in the venture capital arena) will make loans with warrants. These loans have detachable stock options. In other words, if their loan is paid off they will still have the option to buy stock in your company. These profit-seeking organizations invest in a broad range of industries. They use their own capital as well as money borrowed from the SBA. Although they are in a position to provide financing to small businesses in the form of equity securities and long-term loans, they also have to operate within the guidelines that are set by SBA.

A percentage of these companies look for small businesses that have new products or services, which reflect a strong growth potential. There are others that specialize in a field in which their management is competent. Then again, there are also some that focus solely on small businesses that are owned by socially or economically disadvantaged persons. Small businesses as defined by SBA are eligible for SBIC financing. SBA considers a business small when its net worth is $18 million or less, and its average net (after tax) income for the preceding two years does not exceed $6 million.

Should you desire to pursue SBIC financing, you should investigate the types of investments it makes, how much money they have available for investment, and how much might be available in the future. Another consideration is whether they can offer you management services should you require it. When approaching an SBIC, be sure that your business plan is tight and detailed. Your initial presentation will play a major role in your success in obtaining financing. For those of you who still feel left out in the cold, keep reading.

Venture Capital

The Swashbuckler in the financial arena is the venture capitalist. Venture capital is associated with high risk. Although the venture capitalist isn't afraid of eating a pound of raw meat, he will still run your business plan through the traps in an effort to find ways of diluting the risk. These companies are money motivated and will want a reward equivalent to the risk that they are taking. In the past, they have invested in companies that would potentially yield a high rate of return within five to seven years. Due to today's Internet fast paced environment, the time period has been reduced to two to three years with a much higher rate of return.

It is possible for one to find a finance company that will make loans at a high interest rate, but you will not receive the management assistance that is possible with the venture capitalist. A venture capital company can bring additional brainpower to the table. Because they are motivated to protect their interest, they will seek a higher level of involvement in your business. You will be considered a partner and they will help you to achieve your goals. The venture capitalist is an important source of equity for start-up companies. They are professionally managed firms that are generally private partnerships, or closely held corporations. They receive their funds from private and public pension funds, foundations, endowment funds, wealthy individuals, foreign investors and the venture capitalists themselves. Often they will join with other venture firms to fund a project.

A venture capitalist's involvement with your company can vary. Most of them, however, will take the position as passive advisers. They will probably sit on the board of directors and periodically attend a monthly management meeting. Some will take a more active role, however, and desire to help run your business. He or she will probably show up on a weekly basis, and perhaps supply part of the management team. This may not be a bad situation as they can bring a significant amount of resources to the table. They have the ability to pull from a bag of experience that contains ideas gained from helping other companies with similar challenges. Venture capital funds have nurtured many of America's Fortune 500 companies. Don't be intimidated by the venture capital companies, they are approachable, but busy people. I personally give this group a thumb up! In spirit, they are entrepreneurs first and financiers second. They represent the pulse of American Enterprise.

The Wealthy Individual

There are individuals with considerable wealth that will possibly fund your venture. In the lending community, these people are called "angel investors". Some of these individuals will provide capital as well as the expertise required to help develop your business. They may be either wealthy people with management expertise, or retired business people who seek the opportunity to mentor. Angels are not the easiest people to find, but keep your ear to the tracks, as one might be living around the corner. Dealing one on one with the wealthy individual can also be a dangerous path to follow. As illustrated in my story involving the Branson deal, You can find yourself in a financial bind. If not careful you can find yourself dancing with a highly unscrupulous individual. Unless you personally know one of these individuals, I would advise you to focus on the professionals. They are easier to check out and their knowledge and contact base can enhance the success of your business.

The Kneecap Capital

Don't even think about it!

Proceed With Confidence—Proceed With Caution

I have stated on several occasions that you must be careful in your pursuit to find a funding source. Unfortunately, you will be swimming in shark infested waters and it is important for you to scrutinize the funding source with the same vigor that they use to investigate you. This is a two way street.

After you decide which type of company is best for you, your next step is to find one that is located near your place of business. Snoop out the town and ask others if they are credible or not. Don't be afraid to ask the financier for a client list and bank references. Get on the phone and contact some of their clients. Find out if the financier is easy to work with and how they handle adversities. Remember, after you get their money, you will be married for a period of time and an annulment in the world of finance is not an option.

In your search for capital you will run into the independent financial broker. Although some of these individuals can do a good job for you, I advise you to proceed with extreme caution. There are many horror stories of entrepreneurs that have paid fees and received nothing in return. Refuse to pay any up front fees! Request that the broker take his fees out of the closing. Also, you must be careful in negotiating the fee. Remember that until you actually hammer out the deal with the funding source, you will not know how much you will have to give up. Most brokers will ask for a percentage of the funds that they raise. This fee can range from one percent to ten percent. The standard formula is based on the Lehman Theory, which is "five-four-three-two-one." This formula allows the broker to receive five percent of the first million that he raises, four percent of the second million, three percent of the third million, etc. If the funding amount is less than a million, the fee will usually be higher. Committing to give a broker a set percentage will limit your space for negotiation with the funding source. The lender/investor will also show concern if the broker is to receive a large amount of money when the money could be going into the coffers of the business. Should you choose to use a broker, check him out and make sure he is capable of performing.

Once you have identified the type of financing and funding source that you are seeking, you will need to prepare a presentation. You must show that an investment in your company is viable. The best way to do this is by presenting a detailed and comprehensive business plan. Take the time and not only learn how to prepare a professional presentation, but also understand why certain elements are addressed in the proposal. This knowledge will get you through the interview with relative ease. You must get into the funding source's head. Do not let your lifelong dream end up in some financier's wastepaper basket. If you are serious about going into business, I suggest that you pay particular attention to the next section "The Business Plan". In this section I offer suggestions on how to structure your endeavor and what to expect during the interview with the financier.

THE BUSINESS PLAN

Your Track to Run On

It's Easier to Get There When You Know Where You Are Going.

What does your idea look like on paper? Does it grab the reader and entice her to get out the checkbook? As you write your business plan you should be focused on capturing the interest of a potential lender or investor. If this is to happen, then you must be both a technician and artist, paying close attention to structure as well as content. Your plan should convey excitement and constantly sell the reader on your idea's uniqueness. A well-prepared business plan will define your short and long range goals. It is a compass that will help you to achieve these goals and, as with any compass, should be studied and re-accessed regularly. The plan should show how you will get customers and also include marketing strategies. Your business plan is not only your track to run on, it is also your selling tool which is the key to obtaining the financing you need to make your business a success! The process of getting a small business financed can be involved and complicated. If you have engineered your idea into a well thought out plan, you will be prepared to meet the funding source head on and reduce the risk of rejection. Your business plan should answer a multitude of questions and address those elements on which the financial community will base their decisions. Your business plan must be written in a manner that will convince the lender/investor that you and your management team can not only materialize the idea, but also make money in the process.

There are numerous formats available on today's market for developing a business plan. There is also software available, which will enable you to plug in data, and, at the touch of a button, spit out an outline that will guide your future. I have prepared many business plans, not only for my own projects, but also as a consultant for other entrepreneurs. My experience as an appraiser, as well as owning my own mortgage brokerage company has enabled me to rub shoulders with people in the financial community. It has afforded me the opportunity to evaluate their thought process and what is going on in the back room. The people that make up the financial industry live under the heavy burden of possibly losing tremendous sums of money; a terrifying thought. In other words, they are understandably paranoid and often under a great deal of stress. Your business plan should be written with this in mind. They are constantly snooping out projects with strong money making potential. They are extremely proficient when it comes to reviewing a business plan. They will immediately spot the plan that was developed from one of the many software programs that are on the market. These programs offer little uniqueness and will more than likely be trashed.

Although some of these software programs offer more than a thumbnail sketch of a business, the financier is more likely to place his bet on the entrepreneur that has taken the time and effort to develop a business plan that has more substance. There are many critical elements within a business plan that make it next to impossible to plug in certain data about your idea and expect a comprehensive report to appear with the click of a button. The feeling in the financial community is that the entrepreneur will run the enterprise in the same plug and play manner, thus providing a better chance of failure. Although there are some great tasting cake mixes that come out of a box, the distinct taste of grandma's OLE "made from scratch" recipe always steals the show. The business plan format that I have outlined in this book is the result of numerous conversations with people in the financial industry as well as a catalog of successful plans that I have reviewed.

The financial community moves in the fast lane and involves constant decision-making. They must review new proposals on a daily basis and simultaneously baby-sit existing businesses that they have already funded. Because of this tremendous workload, the financier will often request that you send only an executive summary. If he or she is interested in your endeavor, you will be contacted and asked to send the rest of the business plan. Your executive summary should be accompanied by a short cover letter that will basically state the following: *Please find attached a brief review of the financing that I am seeking. If you find this type of project appealing, I will be glad to send you a comprehensive business plan.* The executive summary is a preface to your business plan and is usually no more than three pages long. I advise you to prepare a persuasive executive summary and attach it to your business plan even if you are requested to send it by itself. It is important to get the lender while he is hot. Should the financier have an appetite for your summary he can continue reviewing the entire plan.

The financier is trying to ascertain within as few pages as possible, the content of your business. In this regard, the executive summary is the most important part of the business plan; it should entice the financier to read further. Pay particular attention to this summary. It should show polish and excellence. Make it stand out with excitement. Labor over it and pay close attention to every detail. Let someone with analytical skills read it over, perhaps your banker or accountant. Get some fresh ideas and as much feedback as you possibly can. It is also imperative that you produce the business plan yourself. If you do choose to utilize a consultant, be sure to get involved and do the research yourself. After all, it is you who will be sweating blood during the interview. Realize that no other person will be able to communicate your idea with the same enthusiasm as you.

It is not uncommon for the physician to carry the burden of being an overall problem solver. For some reason, there are people who think that they really know. In the business world many attorneys and accountants also carry this torch. Some attorneys and accountants really are good businessmen, but most are experts at practicing law or crunching numbers. The involvement of your attorney, or accountant in the preparation of your business plan should be limited to reviewing the legalities of your pursuit or to fine tune or tweak your projections. I also advise you to leave them at home when you go to your interview with the financier. If you are unable to determine if a deal is good or bad, then perhaps you should get yourself a job. Your future, as well as the future of others will be riding on your decision-making ability.

The following is an outline of an executive summary and business plan. It also addresses what should be included in its components. It is important for you to know why a financier is asking certain questions. This knowledge will provide assistance and instill confidence when you are called in for a personal interview. In this regard, I will point out the "why" throughout this outline.

Executive Summary

Legal Entity:

Provide the name of your company. Include all of the particulars: your address, phone number, fax and e-mail if you are on-line.

Contact:

If not you, someone who is familiar with your business plan should be the contact person. Be sure that the caller will be able to leave a message if the contact person is not available. It is also advisable to make known the best time to reach this person.

Business Classification:

Summarize the type of business you are pursuing, or involved in. Example: Manufacturing, Distribution, Communications, Wholesale Trade, Retail Medical Related, New Technologies, Hi-Technologies, Construction, Service Related, etc. This section cuts to the chase. There are some industries in which the financier will immediately shy away from.

Business Description:

In a few paragraphs or less, give a condensed summary of your company's activities. Supply the reader with a brief history, if your company is already existing. Remember that this is a summary and you will have the opportunity to expand on everything in the text of your business plan. Grab their attention in this section, make it exciting, but in as few words as possible. If not, the lender might not proceed to read any further. There is usually a trashcan near his or her desk.

Management:

As stated earlier, management can determine the success or failure of a business. The reviewer of your plan is going to dedicate some heavy breathing to this section. Give a brief description of management personnel and emphasize their experience in the industry. This should be a brief section, as the financier will take time to scrutinize the players during the due diligence process. Full length, comprehensive resumes should also be attached to your business plan.

Product/Service:

This section should address what kind of product or service you desire to market. Give a brief description and state why your product or service will outshine your competition. The financier will not be impressed with a company void of special characteristics.

Competition:

This section should not be more than a few paragraphs. List the particular slot your product or service will occupy in the industry. This section will be developed at length in the business plan. Briefly describe your competitors.

Requested Amount:

Specify the exact amount of funding you are trying to raise. If you put in a range, the financier will think that you are uncertain and haven't done your homework, so be specific. Also state what type of financing you desire (equity, or debt). If you are willing to negotiate in this area, then make a statement that you are open to suggestion.

Use of Capital:

Provide a synopsis of how you are going to use the money. This section will be covered in detail later in the business plan. Be careful not to make the potential funding source think that they are merely funding a job for you. Include the dollar amount that will be allocated for salaries and also seize the opportunity to communicate the profit potential of the company. Constantly remind them that much more money will be coming in than going out.

Exit Strategy:

Contrary to belief, the institutional financier does not want to marry you and stay with you for the life of your business. They are in the business of putting out money and receiving capital gains on that money. They will be looking for a way out. If you are seeking debt financing (a loan), the loan documents will spell out the maturity of the loan, thus showing an exit for the financier. If, however, you are seeking equity capital, the funding source will want to know when they will be able to get out of the deal. The exit strategy is an important part of your business plan and should be given considerable thought. A venture capitalist, for example, will want to go public within a short period of time. If this is possible, then sell it as a viable option.

At this point it should be obvious that although the executive summary can be sent to the potential funding source as a probe, it is also a part of the entire business plan. It is imperative to realize that the potential funding source will determine their involvement in your project utilizing four basic elements: 1. Profit potential 2. Strength of management 3. Special characteristics 4. Exit strategy. If these elements do not stand center stage and take a bow in your executive summary, then go back to the drawing board and rewrite it!

Before we get into the meat of business plan development, let's discuss a few other matters. First of all, how much capital do you really need? Remember that the more you borrow, the more collateral will be required should you seek debt capital. If you are requesting equity financing, the more that you receive, the more equity ownership you will have to give up to the funding source. You will, however, need to secure enough funds to take you through various stages of progress. Remember the different stages of funding? If you raise startup funds and have to go back into the trough to get expansion capital, you will have to give up another arm, or elbow. I shall now make another effort to drill this into your head. The Funding Source Is In Business To Make Money! The more often that you go back to them, the more you are going to have to pay. So spend a little more time and make it leak proof. Pencil it out until the lead breaks. You will thank yourself in the long run.

A table can be utilized as an aid to help you determine the amount of capital that you need for a start-up business. You will, of course, need to make additions and deletions depending on your circumstance: "See table 3." This concludes the basic elements of the executive summary. Now we shall get into the meat of the business plan.

Business Concept

In this section you will give a clear description of what kind of business you are in. Take your time and focus on this section, it will force you to gain more knowledge about your business than you previously had. It is also good practice to assume that the financier knows nothing about your business. Be a good professor and educate them about your business. Although this section is industry related, it is important to point out the features in your business that have special characteristics. Remember, you must constantly sell the unique qualities of your business, as the financier will not be interested in another "Me Too" company.

Company Profile:

Just in case your executive summary is sent out separate from your business plan or misplaced, this section is a repeat of the company and contact information that is previously listed. Record the name of your company, address, telephone numbers, contact person, etc. Many funding sources will also like to see the SIC code which reflects the industry that you are in. The National Bureau of Standards has codebooks that list SIC numbers. Your local library, as well as the Internet, will offer great assistance to you as you build your business plan.

Overview of Your Business:

Provide the reader with a description of your company, the product and/or service. This section is relatively short, as the components of your business will be drawn out in the rest of the plan. You should give the financier enough sizzle to entice him to read further. You can state, for example, that your company designs, manufactures and markets sport foot-ware and apparel. Again, you can briefly insert any special characteristics that your company has to offer.

Historical Overview:

In this section you should identify at what stage of funding you are. Is your company in the start-up phase, expansion stage or positioning itself for an initial public offering? If your business is a start-up company, void of history, then paint a word picture beginning with the idea or concept, and describe its evolution to its present state. If it is an existing company, however, you should outline its business history. Give dates and background such as when it was established, and when certain benchmarks were achieved. The funding source will draw most of this information out of you when you are up close and personal, so this section can be brief and to the point.

Future Objectives:

The funding source is always trying to get a clear mental picture of what your goals are, and your method of getting from your present state to substantial profits. Utilize this section to give them a clear picture of the forecasted future. Your projections will be highly scrutinized in terms of how reachable they are. If you don't have realistic milestones that are obtainable, it is possible for both you and the investor to lose your footing. Your projections will answer the following questions: Where will you be five years from now? When will you break-even, and at what point will you realize a positive cash flow? If you have plans to introduce another product or service in a few years, discuss it here. This section should be a narrative summation that supports your projections. It should be exciting and show the funding source that you can run a stable company and at the same time, feed the greed need for the both of you.

Special Features:

Financiers get hit with "me too" companies on a regular basis. They are looking for something that meets an unfulfilled need in a particular area. What niche is your company involved in that makes it rise above your competitors? What are you doing that is different, better, faster or newer than everyone else? Is your product or marketing concept unique? Do you have something that has extraordinary appeal to the customer? Perhaps your management team is special. Remember that the funding source is looking at many other investments. What makes your company stand out? Why is it so special? Use this opportunity to sell your company. Perhaps your business position in the marketplace is unique due to a patent or trademark. It is more profitable for an idea to provide a solution to an existing need, rather than supply a product or service in hopes of creating the need and demand for the idea.

Product/Service:

What is your product or service? Describe the benefits from the customer's point of view. How much is your product going to cost and how did you determine this price? Did you extract it from the market by utilizing comparable prices from various competitors? Was your pricing strategy based upon percentage markup on cost? Is it high, or low due to your location? Are your prices in line with your image? What is the percentage of profit margin that you have allowed for? If you have several products, describe each one separately and the cost to the customer. What steps have you taken or intend to pursue to protect the proprietary nature of your product? Have you obtained a patent? Have you prepared non-disclosure/non-circumvent agreements for other parties to sign? What are the advantages of your product or service?

Customer Base:

Who are your customers and why will they buy your product or service? Do they come from the private sector, or are they wholesalers? Is your product or service inexpensive? Does your product address a medical condition presently in vogue, or fit within the wave of a new fad? Give all of the reasons why customers will buy your product or service. Also, discuss how long the customer will remain loyal and for what reason? Include what customer services you will provide.

Industry/Market:

Give a synopsis of the marketplace for your product. Demonstrate that you are extremely knowledgeable when discussing your industry. Where is your industry going? What are the current conditions of your industry? Why are the current market distributions the way they are? Explain to the financier the details of industry sales and how your product will penetrate the industry. What is the anticipated timeline for initial market penetration and how much capital will be needed to acquire this initial share? When you analyze the marketplace you should include the total dollar volume and its growth rate. What is the overall demand for your product? For example: 1997 industry sales reached $1,000,000; in 1998 there was a ten-percent increase to $1,100,000. You can include projected sales, but you will need to support any assumptions that you make in regards to the market. If your product has a limited position in the marketplace, make sure that your analysis is congruent.

The industry sales should reflect your niche market and not the entire marketplace. In other words, if you are selling sport footwear, your industry should not reflect the entire footwear industry to include tuxedo shoes, women's high heels, work-boots, etc. Your market penetration will be in the leisure footwear arena. Is your target market domestic or international? The funding source will want to know as much as possible about your industry. The more you include in your business plan, the less time it will take for the due diligence process. Make it as easy as possible for the funding source by supplying them with a list of the major publications associated with your industry. As much as possible, you should help the financier understand the industry. Provide references to all trade associations. Material supplied by these organizations will also help support statements and assumptions that you have made throughout your business plan, so take advantage of it.

Competitors:

This is an area in which you need to show off your knowledge. After all, your competitors can put you and the financier in the grave. Show that you have snooped out all of those companies who offer competitive or related products or services. List those who offer complementary products in the same or similar industries. Provide a brief profile on your competitors to include the following: name, address, years in business, product, price of product, market-share. Show how strong your competitors are in the marketplace. Is your product more marketable because theirs is obsolete? Show why it is possible for you to be a strong contender among your competition. Compare your strengths and weaknesses to that of your competitors. Consider elements such as location, size of resources, reputation, services, personnel, etc. What has your competition done to obtain their market share? Is it possible to form a future, strategic partnership with a competitor? Your funding source will find a certain comfort level if possible exit solutions have been worked out just in case the plan drifts off course. You will find it difficult to convince the financier that there is no competition out there, but if you feel that you have an isolated niche, then make a strong argument in that regard. It's the kind of uniqueness that will stimulate interest.

Marketing:

How will you get your product from the factory to the end user? Will you have distributors? Will you use Tele-marketers? A direct sales force? How will you sell your product? List your channels of distribution. The funding source will sweat and itch a great deal if he sees that your market is dependent upon one customer such as the government. It will also send him scurrying for a glass of water if you have a strong dependence on one broker or intermediary. Explain in detail any special marketing arrangement. Make the financier feel comfortable with your market strategy. Take him through it step by step so that he will thoroughly understand. If you have a grandiose marketing scheme in mind that might spook the financier, leave it out of your proposal. In other words, you don't want to tell a financier that you are going to train a team to go to the Olympics so they can be seen wearing your product in front of the world. You will send him into convulsions! Remember that his concerns should also be yours!

Production:

How are you going to get your product manufactured and how much will it cost you? Address any economic factors that could affect your product or service. Consider things such as industry health, economic trends, and rising prices. Does your product use a raw material in which other elements can drastically affect the cost of production? Oil prices, for example, could raise the price of a plastic product and put a company out of business if operating on a narrow margin. List all of the elements that could cause a significant price change. Remember that production cost is the key factor in pricing out your product to the end user. How complicated is the production process? Are specially skilled employees required? Think in global as well as domestic terms. The funding source needs to feel comfortable that a domino won't fall in Saudi Arabia and collapse an enterprise that sells sneakers in Nebraska. Lenders and investors are constantly viewing the economic weather channel.

Labor:

State the number of people, if any, that you currently employ. How difficult is it to acquire and maintain your work force? If you have a start-up business, how many employees do you anticipate you will have in the future? Are you going to require union, or non-union workers? If your employees are union, describe the contract and list its expiration date. Are your employees blue or white-collar workers? If you are in an area where it is a challenge to maintain employees, the financier will want to know how you plan to deal with the problem.

Suppliers:

List the companies that supply or will supply you with the raw materials that you will require. List several of your major suppliers, the items that they supply and the dollar volume. If you are a start-up company, a list of potential suppliers, the items and the forecasted dollar volume should be provided. The funding source needs to determine the stability of the suppliers as well as the endurance of associated costs.

Equipment:

Supply a list of the equipment you will need to run your business. Research the availability of this equipment and include this information in this section. Is there a backlog in terms of delivery? If your company is successful will it be possible to acquire additional equipment within a reasonable length of time? Are employees with special skills needed to operate this equipment? If so, are they readily available? Do you plan on buying the equipment or leasing it? If you are putting this equipment up for collateral, how easily can it be liquidated? In other words, how strong is your collateral? The financier will see all equipment as potential collateral.

Real Estate:

What is the size of your facility? Is it large enough to accommodate growth? In this section, list the size of your facility and the price per square foot. If you are leasing or intend to lease, describe the crucial elements of the agreement. The funding source will look at your five-year forecast and determine if the facility is capable of accommodating the expected size of your company five years from now. The funding source will look at you with raised eyebrows if it appears that you will have to move at a time when you are active and thriving. It will also show that you have not thought your plan out very well.

Patents, Trademarks and Copyrights:

It is nearly impossible to predict the success of any new product due to the complexity and constantly changing trends of the marketplace. Without protection, however, your chance of success greatly diminishes. If you have a patent or trademark, use this section to highlight the special characteristics of your product and its unique position in the marketplace. If you are in the process of obtaining these elements it is important to let the funding source know at what stage you are currently.

Research and Development:

If you require Research and Development funds, take your time and construct this section carefully. This is an area that can put the funding source in the fetal position. Define in detail what you are trying to accomplish with the R&D funds. How much has already been spent? How much more time and money will be required for this phase? Remember that the funding source (and so should you) wants to get the product developed and into the hands of the consumer in the least amount of time utilizing the least amount of capital. Does the product require regulatory approval? Are there any foreseeable delays that could affect your timetable? Do you have a back-up plan if tests, approvals, or patents don't go as expected? Research and development always breeds a concern that the R&D will never end and significantly eat into capital and profit margin.

Legal Issues:

The key to the success of any business endeavor is integrity. Give the names of any snakes that you have living in your closet. If you are being sued, or in the process of suing another entity, you should reveal the conditions in this section of your business plan. Such issues eventually come out in the due diligence stage and can be both embarrassing for you as well as the funding source. Be advised that the funding source will be uncomfortable if you have a second home in the courtroom. Clear the decks and discuss it up front. They also understand that this is not a perfect world and that sometimes things happen. Provide a detailed explanation, pray for forgiveness and promise to sin no more.

Government Rules and Regulations:

Although rules and regulations are a necessity in today's society, they can sometimes cause great strain on businesses. If you are in a business that is regulated by Uncle Sam, utilize this section to explain the regulations and your relationship with the government. The funding source can probably tell you many stories of businesses that have failed due to governmental red tape. Remember, when you fail, so do they. Expect the funding source to proceed with caution.

Insurance:

In this part of your business plan the funding source is interested in what kind of insurance coverage will cushion your company from any unexpected blows. Health insurance and key man insurance are examples of what could be significant to the operation of your business. Think of your insurance needs and list them all.

Company Structure:

How did you structure your business? Describe the legal entity existence of your company. If your company is a corporation, list what type of corporation, when it was incorporated, and where. If it is a partnership give the details of your partnership agreement.

Management/Personnel

Key Personnel:

As stated throughout this book, this section is extremely important to the funding source. The background and experience of the management team will be analyzed from all angles. Never let your guard down, as management will be under constant evaluation, whether it is during the interview, phone conversations or at the bowling alley. In this section, list all of the key employees and include a brief biography (a short paragraph on each person). The funding source would like to see a group of achievers that display a high degree of integrity. Lenders and investors have all experienced those entrepreneurs that have larceny in their hearts. The issue of honesty is one that you must not dance around with. If there has been something in the past that might be of concern, then put it on the table and explain the situation. An honest explanation regarding the series of events, in itself, can show fidelity. If your credit report makes you look like you've been running with Bonnie and Clyde, give a detailed explanation. You should also list the principal shareholders and any possible conflicts of interest. Lay everything out on the table in a neat little pile.

Consultants:

Provide the names, addresses, and phone numbers of any consultants who have provided you services. If it is not self-explanatory, give a brief explanation of the services they have provided and if any payment balances to them are outstanding.

Financial Data

The funding source will view this section as a starting point for negotiations. It will help determine what kind of financing will be acceptable to both of you.

Proposed financing

Debt Financing:

This type of financing is normally easier and cheaper to obtain than equity funding. If your desire is to obtain a loan, utilize this section to discuss the terms. Provide the interest rate that you have in mind. Ask yourself if it is reasonable in regards to the risk that you are asking the financier to take. Remember that debt financing usually requires monthly payments, whether or not you have reached the stage of positive cash flow. Do you require a period in which you will be making payments on the interest only? If so, why? New equipment or other acquired assets will take time to begin paying for themselves. An initial period of interest only or skip payments may be needed to offset your lack of cash flow. At what point can you begin to repay the loan? Will the interest rate be fixed, or adjustable? Remember that with a fixed rate you know where you stand, but with an adjustable rate you are playing futuristic roulette. Rates will modulate as you add or subtract risk. Prime rate plus one to three percent is normal. If LIBOR (London Index) is utilized as the basis, plus three to five percent is normal. The term of your loan should be based upon your financial projections, or the useful life of the asset you are financing. Receivable and contract financing are usually less than a year, whereas equipment is normally one to five years. Real estate and other long-term assets range from five to twenty years. If you are not sure of this area, then list some parameters and provide an ending statement that will inform the lender that you are open to suggestions. Before you go into the interview, ask yourself the following questions: How much debt can I afford? If interest rates rise, or if my cash flow is off, will I still be able to handle my obligations? Am I willing to pledge company and personal assets and give a personal guarantee? Know the answers to these questions before you go in.

Equity Financing:

Equity investors put their money on the table gambling for high returns. Although they expect little or no return in the early stages, they anticipate that projections and benchmarks be met. Naturally, they will desire to take a much larger share of a start-up company, than a company that has a successful track record. There are certain questions that you should consider. If you are selling common stock, what price will the investor pay? Will there be any restrictions on the shares? Will the investor have voting rights? Will there be a dividend? If you have to return the investor's money, will you have to redeem (convert into cash) the common stock? What is the exercise price for any option offered and how was the price determined? What will be the coupon value for any preferred stock? Can preferred stock be converted into common stock? Will there be voting rights on the preferred stock? Will I be able to keep up with all of the required reporting? How comfortable am I about disclosing company secrets to potential investors? Again, if you are open to suggestions in the area, let the funding source know in this section of your business plan. If you are a little fuzzy on debt and equity financing, brush up on it as best you can. Read! Study! Read some more until you have a thorough understanding.

Collateral:

What collateral do you have available to make the lender feel comfortable? How much is it worth? How did you determine its value? Do you have a recent appraisal? If you are void of collateral it is necessary to mention this in this part of the business plan. I have known investors that made their commitment based on the strength of the project only. There are also sources that for a fee will put up collateral for a project. If you don't have all of the components needed for financing, don't lay down at the first obstacle. Keep trying! Find a way to make it work.

Reporting:

Some investors will want monthly financial statements and updated projections. If you are willing to provide reports, mention it in this part of your plan. You should have these reports on hand for your own personal use. Why not provide them to the source that is instrumental in making your endeavor work?

Use of Capital:

How are you going to use the money? Be specific; spell out all areas in which you will spend the money, the dollar amount and the justification for each expenditure. Consider what immediate bills need to be paid. What equipment is initially required? How much is needed for raw materials and payroll? Your cash flow model should be month to month for one year and quarterly for the next four years.

Ownership:

If you are seeking equity financing and the investor will own some of the company, spell out how much ownership this source will have. Additionally, define in this section how much ownership will be distributed to key management. Remember that management has to own enough to stay motivated and the investor has to have enough incentive to waltz up to the altar.

Associated Risks:

In this section, the financier will play the devils advocate and run your plan through the sewer. He will once again pull out his bad experience pouch and ask you all of the "what if" questions. Some of these questions can be quite annoying, but there is probably a good reason that they are being asked. This is not the time to use sarcasm or get cute. Just answer the questions with enthusiasm and keep a positive mental attitude. Concentrate on keeping his feet warm!

Operating History:

You do not want the funding source to verbally sweep you off of your feet during the interview. Utilize this section to address the "What If" questions. You will probably be asked them anyway, but you will be rehearsed enough to fire back your rebuttal. You will be asked if this is your first company that you are starting and why do you think that you will be successful? How will you handle the hand grenades that are occasionally tossed into a new company? Be sure to throw your management team into the mix. Explain that they are capable of putting out fires specific to their particular skills. If your management team is limping in certain areas, mention that there are numerous outside consultants that can be tapped into. In this section of your business plan, explain in detail how you will handle potential challenges and you won't be knocked-out cold during the interview.

Uncertainties:

How can the competition pull the carpet out from under you? What economic demons can destroy your company? Are there any new products around the corner that could place you in the back seat? How solid is your marketing plan? Address all of these questions in this section. Be prepared to get hit with the many questions that the funding source will pull out of his bad experience pouch. If you have a new product, the funding source will also spend a lot of time pacing the floor. If your business is a new production facility, the financier will break out his ulcer medicine. If you have never run a production facility before, it is imperative that you acquire key management that has. You must also convince the financier that you have priced everything out correctly. Write down what you see as potential challenges and spell out how you will alleviate them. Remember that the financier's bad experiences can also provide insight to problem solving. If he tells you a war story, ask how he dealt with the issue.

Dependence on Key Personnel:

If a truck hits the key person or pillar that is holding up the company, what are you going to do? In this section, address how you will handle the doomsday scenario. Key man insurance is a way to eliminate some of the pain. Give a lot of thought to this section and be prepared to be questioned again in the interview. Remember that you are dealing with paranoid people. Try not to upgrade their condition to Alzheimer's.

Return on Investment and Exit

This part of your plan is short and to the point. It deals primarily with your projections. In narrative form it spells out the bottom line. How much is the profit potential to the investor and how long is the marriage going to last? Is the product or service in such a demand that it will be feasible for the company to go public? Have you discussed this with a brokerage firm and established an estimate using comparable companies? Is the sale of your company a consideration? What is the market like? Is it possible to gain independence by purchasing back the investor's shares? If so, what method will be utilized to establish value? Perhaps an agreed upon, predetermined amount will satisfy the investor. If debt capital is what you have chosen, will the business generate a cash flow large enough to support the debt? The answer to these questions will also help narrow your search for the source most likely to fund your venture.

Proforma Analysis:

Your projections will be based upon certain assumptions. In this section, you will need to spell them out. The funding source has more than likely seen many plans in which the entrepreneur looked skyward and based the projections on thin air. You will be pretty safe if you extract your assumptions from the market. Look at comparable companies that are in your industry and base your data on what the market is doing. Remember that the investors return on investment is directly related to the accuracy of your projections. Your financial projections should be clear, concise, logical and supportable. They are one of the most scrutinized elements in securing financing for your endeavor. The funding source will spend many hours dissecting your assumptions.

Ratio Analysis:

When evaluating your projections, the investor is going to look for any discrepancies. Utilize this section to explain certain inconsistencies before you meet with the funding source. Your gross margins should increase each year as your company grows (gross profit margin is calculated by dividing the gross profits by the total net sales). If this margin for some reason undulates, then explain why. If payroll expenses as a percentage show a substantial increase, address it in this section.

Financial Statements:

In this part of your plan you should attach a copy of your financial statements. If your company is a start-up venture and not existing, attached a copy of your personal financial statement. If your personal financial statement is weak or on death row, go back through your business plan. Make the plan strong enough to focus the financier's attention away from this section. You've come this far. Hit the damn grand slam!

Projections:

In this part of your business plan attach your assumptions and financial projections. This is a section, which you should study and know like the back of your hand. I suggest that you do your own projections and then let a CPA review it to see if it is reasonable and put it into an acceptable format.

Product Literature:

At this point you can attach any information that will assist the financier in understanding your endeavor. Attach any information, which will encourage the financier to do business with you. If you have a credibility issue, attach letters of support and a list of references to help clear it up.

Table 1

Standards and Ratios

Margins & Ratios	Acceptable Standard	Explanations/Formulas
Gross Profit Margin	60% or Higher	Gross sales minus cost of goods sold
Net Profit Margin	10% or Higher	Gross sales to net income
Debt to Worth Ratio	3 to 1 or Higher	Creditors capital to owners capital
Debt Coverage Ratio	1.25 to 1 or Higher	Net income divided by debt payment (principal & Interest).
A/R Turnover Ratio	Close to 12	Gross sales divided by accounts receivable
Current Ratio	1 to 1 or Higher	Current assets divided by current liabilities
Quick Ratio	0.5 to 1 or Higher	Current assets minus inventory divided by current liabilities

Table 2

SBA Express Size Standards

TYPE OF BUSINESS	SIZE STANDARDS
Manufacturing	From 500 to 1500 employees
Wholesaling	100 employees
Services	From $2.5 million to $21.5 million in annual receipts
Retailing	From $5 million to $21 million in annual receipts
General Construction	From $13.3 million to $17 million in annual receipts

Table 3

Determining amount of funds required

One Time Start-up Costs		Monthly Expenses	
Fixtures and equipment	$	Salary of owner / manager	$
Installation of Fixtures & equip	$	All other wages	$
Decorating and Remodeling	$	Rent	$
Deposits with public utilities	$	Advertising	$
Starting Inventory	$	Supplies	$
Legal & other professional fees	$	Telephone	$
Licenses & permits	$	Utilities	$
Advertising & opening promotions	$	Insurance	$
Consulting & software	$	Taxes, including Social Security	$
Cash	$	Interest	$
Other	$	Maintenance	$
		Legal & other professional fees	$
		Miscellaneous	$
		Calculate total start-up funds	$
		Estimate months needed to gear up	$

EPILOGUE

I have tried to compile a lighthearted recount of some of my greatest business blunders. I believe that if I had this book as a business partner and companion while in the trenches, I would have made quicker and wiser decisions. It has been my intent to give you a few laughs and a few lessons as well. Hopefully, this book will inspire you to make one more call, perhaps summon up the gumption to bang on the table, or even kick in the door to get what you want.

Going into business involves taking risk and risking failure. Your ability to know when to stop, shift focus, or continue in a different direction can make or break you. You define the moment in your own terms and whatever your predicament, you are always going to be where you think you are. I hope that this book will help you to analyze everything very carefully and precisely, build scientifically on that bedrock and then go with your gut feeling. I urge you to prepare your business plan utilizing the tools outlined in this book, draw yourself up to your full height, and put on a vintage performance. I wish you enjoyment and good luck while following your aspirations and manipulating your dreams.

Conclusions

Approaching the Altar

The altar can be a very scary place if one is not prepared. It represents commitment. Once you have done your homework and know how the financial industry works, however, your fear should be somewhat neutralized. With a comprehensive business plan in your possession, you should be able to make your approach with confidence. Thorough knowledge of your business plan is a necessity, this includes the assumptions and financial projections which basically outlines how much money can be made in the marriage. You must convince the financier that you know what you are talking about. The best way to do this is to really know. Also remember that once you are at the negotiation table, you do not have to say, "I do" if it doesn't feel right. If you are mentally and emotionally prepared to get up and walk out of the room should the deal fail to meet your criteria, you will be free of the stress and anxiety that often loiters around the negotiation table. Make sure that you have the terms that you are seeking well defined in your mind. Realize that some points are worth fighting for, and some are not. Express your objections and question anything that is not clear. Get everything in writing, even if it is in the form of a letter of understanding. Remember your long-term goals and make sure that your agreements are in line with what you are trying to achieve.

It is important to seek professional counsel before you sign anything. It is better, however, for you to take the paperwork to your attorney rather than bring him to the meeting. You are not there to argue, but to negotiate a deal. Try to pledge as little collateral as possible just in case you need it for future use. If at all possible, avoid any acceleration clauses that have a pre-payment penalty. Also try not to give the financier the right to buy back your stock at a fixed price. Pay particular attention to anything that will have serious long-term effects, such as conditions, covenants, ratios and restrictive clauses. When at the negotiation table, constantly remind yourself that every relationship is based on trust. If that feeling of trust isn't in the room, then don't do the deal.

I hope that this book has given you some education, insight and inspiration. The entrepreneurial spirit is what built America. I wish you all a successful journey that is filled with, abundance, growth and prosperity.

ABOUT THE AUTHOR

Born in 1949, Leamon Cotton, Jr. grew up in Reno, Nevada where he attended the University of Nevada Reno. After honorably serving in the military, he became addicted to high-risk business ventures. This course eventually led him to West Africa where he found himself riding a dirt bike through the rain forest in the pursuit of gold. Keep an eye out for "Liberia" to be published in early 2001.

GLOSSARY

Above the line. In accounting, ordinary items of income and expenditure are treated "above the line," which means they are included in determining "net profit." Extraordinary items are treated "below the line."

Accounts. Every company must keep sufficient records of its transactions for persons to ascertain the company's financial position with reasonable accuracy at any time. These are normally kept at the principal place of business. After the end of each fiscal year the directors are responsible for providing the following financial statements to the shareholders: balance sheet, revenue account, and an auditors' report. This may also require the filing of the statements with the SEC or another regulatory agency.

Accounts payable/receivable. Terms for amounts owing by or to a business.

Acid test. The extent to which a company could meet its current liabilities from current assets other than stock. This is an onerous test of liquidity, which may be inappropriate to normal business practice in many industries.

Ad valorem. Latin term for "according to value." A variable form of tax that is determined according to the price of the object taxed. An ad valorem tax suits revenue authorities better in times of inflation.

Amortization. Reduction of principal of a loan by repaying it in installments, each installment payment including interest.

Appreciation. A rise in value of an asset.

Arm's length. Refers to business transactions where neither the buyer nor the seller is influenced by the other. In a non-arm' length transaction you might sell a family member some assets of the business at a low price to move assets out of the business.

Asset. Property of any kind, real or personal, tangible or intangible.

Current assets. Assets readily converted to cash, that is, cash marketable securities and accounts receivable.

Fixed assets. Assets of a long-term or permanent nature that may be used in the operation of a business or production of income.

Frozen assets. Assets that are illiquid or otherwise difficult to convert to cash.

Authorized capital. With respect to a corporation or company, the sum value of the aggregate of par value of all shares that the company is authorized to issue.

Basis point. One hundredth of 1 percent.

Below the line. In accounting, extraordinary items and appropriations are treated "below the line," which means that they do not form part of the net profit.

Blue sky laws. Common name for U.S. states' (as opposed to federal) laws regulating the sale of securities intended to protect investors.

Board. Meaning board of directors of a corporation. These are the individuals who control a corporation for the benefit of the stockholders.

They listen to management's recommendations and set policy for the corporation.

Boiler plate. Boilerplate paragraphs are the standard paragraphs in most venture capital and investment documents.

Book value. The value at which assets or liabilities are carried on the accounting books.

Bricks and mortar. The assets of your company. The term is derived from a building that is built of bricks and mortar.

Broker. (Money-broker) one who lends or raises money to or for another.

Buy-sell. A buy-sell agreement is one in which, under certain circumstances, the first party in a partnership must agree to buy out the second party, or the second party must agree to buy out the first party. Buy-sell arrangements usually are negotiated between two partners such as an entrepreneur and a venture capitalist.

Buy out. The term refers to the sale of a business; for example, when the buyer of a business buys it, he "buys out" the seller.

Capitalization. The current value of a recurring income or cash flow. The act of computing the value of recurring income or cash flow. A Corporation can determine its market capitalization by multiplying the market price of its shares by the number of outstanding shares.

Cashflow. The most important aspect of any small business is the cash flow. The money coming in and the money going out is the flow of cash that determines whether a business will survive.

Cash in. When you sell all or part of your stock for cash. Cashing in is an extremely exciting moment because it usually means you are rich.

Certificate of deposit (CD). An investment instrument available through a financial institution. Investors agree to deposit a predetermined amount of money in the financial institution for an established period of time (one month, two months, three months, or six months, for example). In return they receive a certificate of deposit. Because they are easily negotiable and generally a safe investment, certificates of deposit usually pay lower rates of interest than riskier investment instruments, such as mutual funds and stocks.

Closing. The event that occurs when you sign legal documents binding your company and transferring cash from the lending source to your company.

Collateral. The assets you pledge for a loan made to your company. If you do not repay the loan, the collateral can be sold.

Commitment fee. Money paid in advance to ensure that you will not back out of a financial arrangement.

Common stock. Ordinary capital shares of a corporation that have claim on the net assets and income of the corporation after all prior or preferred claims have been paid.

Compound interest. The practice of charging interest on unpaid interest in addition to the principal of a loan or deposit.

Consideration. The inducement to enter into a contract, that is, money or price paid or given by one party for the performance of the other.

Control. Owning 51 percent of the stock of a company or, from another perspective, owning enough stock in the company to control what management will do.

Convertible. Usually refers to debt or preferred stock, each of which is convertible into common stock of the company. Obviously, it is possible to have debt convertible into preferred stock and it is even possible to have preferred stock convertible into debt, although the latter is unusual.

Convenant. Paragraphs in the legal documents stating the things you agree you will do and paragraphs stating what you will not do.

Deal. The bargain struck between the lending source and the entrepreneur. In more general terms, any agreement between two individuals, especially a buyer and a seller.

Debenture. Another word for a debt, note, or loan.

Debt service. The amount of money you have to pay on a debt in order to keep it from being in default. If you make the payments that are called for under a note or loan, then you are servicing the debt.

Default. When you have done something you told your investor you would not do, which is written down in the investment agreement, then it is default.

Depreciation. The loss of value from an asset from all causes. In an accounting application, the charge against profits "above the line" to represent the extent that fixed assets have worn out over the year.

Disclosure. Revealing the truth or any other information that is generally not known.

Discounted cash flow. Method of evaluating the future returns on a business venture by considering whether the money could not more profitably be placed on deposit or some other investment.

Dividend. A share of the profits of a company paid to all holders of a class of securities. Dividends on preferred shares are usually paid at a predetermined rate and paid prior to any payment to holders of the company's common stock. Dividends on common stock are generally paid at the rate decided by the company's board of directors.

Downside. The amount of risk an investor takes in any venture is called the downside. If you stand to lose half your money if a business goes under, the downside risk is said to be 50 percent.

Due diligence. The process of investigating a business venture to determine its feasibility.

Earnings. (1) Income. (2) An accounting term for profit attributable to equity shareholders. It therefore combines dividends with retained profits. This may increase as a result of good management or following a takeover that required the issue of many new shares.

Earn out. The contract between the entrepreneur and the buying corporation that provides for the entrepreneur to earn additional money on the sale of his company, if operating earnings are in excess of a specified amount during the future years.

Earnings yield. The amount a company earned on 100 units of currency (for example dollars) over a period. It is the reciprocal of the price earnings (P/E) ratio.

Equity. Normally it describes the preferred and common stock of a business. Also, it is frequently used to describe the amount of ownership of one person or a lender in a business.

Equity kicker. Feature of a loan agreement, whereby the lender will participate in part of the success of the venture to which it is lending in addition to receiving interest and repayment.

Exercise. An option is exercised when the option's owner demands delivery against payment. This may happen at any time during the life of the option.

Exit. The sale of equity or ownership in the business for cash or notes.

Fiduciary. Anyone who is put in a position of trust has a fiduciary duty to perform those tasks loyally and in good faith and not to permit any conflict between his duties and personal interests to those of his principal.

Fixed assets. In accounting, assets that can be expected to reappear on the balance sheet in a year's time more specifically referred to "property, plant, and equipment."

Good idea. A good idea in the lending industry is one that makes a large amount of money.

Good people. The supreme compliment to an entrepreneur by a lender. It means the entrepreneur is honest, loyal, and a straight shooter.

Grace period. The period of time you have to correct a default.

Guarantee. An undertaking from a third party that a loan will be repaid. By law a guarantee must be in writing to be enforceable. A guarantee may be secured by collateral held in escrow.

Insolvent. A person's or company's situation of being unable to pay debts as they fall due.

Internal rate of return. The annual return on an investment expressed as a percentage of the original investment and allowing for the fact that revenues generated in the near future are more valuable than revenues received in the distant future.

Lead investor. The investor who leads a group of investors into an investment. Usually one venture capitalist will be the lead investor when a group of venture capitalists invest in a single business.

Leverage. Another term for debt. Debt is usually referred to as leverage because in using debt, one does not have to give up equity. So for a very small amount of equity and a large amount of debt, one can leverage a business on the basis of its assets.

Leveraged buy-out. An acquisition of a business using mostly debt and a small amount of equity. The assets of the business secure the debt.

Liability. A debt or other obligation owed by a person or corporation. Its usual forms are accounts and notes payable.

Libor (London interbank offered rate). The rate of interest given to a first-class bank in the London interbank market when it makes a loan off another member bank within the market.

Limited liability company (LLC OR LC). Consists of member owners and a manager, at a minimum. Similar to a corporation that is taxed as a partnership or as an S-corporation. It combines the more favorable traits of a corporation and a partnership. The LLC structure permits the complete passthrough of tax advantages and the operational flexibility found in a partnership, operating in a corporate-style structure, with limited liability as provided by the state's laws. The LLC may be managed by members but need not be. A professional company manager may manage it. LLCs are fairly new, without a clear body of case law and firm guidelines.

Options. The right given someone to purchase an asset within a certain timeframe. The right given to a lender to buy stock in your company.

Paper. The notes you receive for the sale of your stock or the assets in your company. These are called paper because paper is fairly worthless. Many of the notes received by entrepreneurs from the sale of their company to someone else have turned into worthless paper.

Partnership. An association of two or more persons to carry on an enterprise for a profit.

General partnership. A partnership in which each partner is a general partner and has personal liability for all partnership debts.

Limited partnership. A partnership with a minimum of one general partner who manages the affairs of the partnership and has personal liability for all partnership debts, and a minimum of one general partner whose liability is limited to its investment buy who has little or no say in the management of the partnership affairs.

Pool. This usually refers to a venture capital limited partnership in which each investor has "pooled' his resources by purchasing a limited partnership interest in the venture capital partnership. The partnership then invests in small businesses.

Preferred stock. The stock of a corporation with priority or preference over the common stock in the distribution of dividends and assets.

Price earnings ratio (PE). The number that is multiplied times the earnings per share number in order to ascertain a fair price for a stock. If a stock is earning $.50 a share and the PE Ratio of eight is used, then the stock is worth $4 per share.

Pricing. The determination as to the price that an investor will pay to purchase shares of stock in the business. Pricing is determined on the basis of the full value of the company. Every time one share of stock is sold, the sale determines the value of the company and in this way, pricing occurs.

Proposal. The document that must be put together by an entrepreneur in order to propose an investment to a lender or other investors.

Public offering. The selling of shares to the general public through the registration of shares with the Securities and Exchange Commission.

Raising capital. Refers to obtaining capital from investors or other lending sources.

Representations. Facts that the entrepreneur reveals about his company that are represented to the lending source as being true.

Situation. A common lending term in regards to any business deal.

Structure. Refers to the type of financing that will be used to fund a small business. The structure might be $200,000 in common stock and $750,000 in debt at 15 percent interest for ten years.

Syndication. The process whereby a group of investors will each put in a portion of the amount of money needed to finance a small business. This is common and tends to spread the associated risks.

Take back. Refers to a situation where a seller of a business must take back something rather than cash. The take back usually refers to a note with reasonable terms and conditions.

Turnaround. Describes businesses that are in trouble and whose management will cause the business to become profitable so they are no longer in a bad situation.

Underwriter. The stockbrokerage house used to raise funds for a small business in a public offering. In a public offering the stockbrokerage house that underwrites the small business is the one that buys the shares from the small business and sells them to the general public.

Unlocking agreement. A legal agreement between two parties meaning that one party may require the other to buy it out under certain conditions; thus, the so-called unlocking of the partnership.

Upside. The amount of money that one can make by investing in a certain deal is called the upside potential.

Warrant. A stock option given to someone else that entitles them to purchase stock in your company.

Warranties. These are items concerning your company that you have told the investor is true.

www.ingramcontent.com/pod-product-compliance
Lightning Source LLC
Chambersburg PA
CBHW030850180526
45163CB00004B/1520